ROMANOFF AND JULIET

A comedy of Russian-American relations during the Cold
War in and around their embassies in a tiny neutral state in
Europe. A young Russian and an American girl fall in love
and so create great embarrassment for their diplomat fathers,
with at last some moderating of the feud.

THE HEREFORD PLAYS

General Editor: E. R. Wood

Maxwell Anderson
Winterset

Robert Ardrey
Thunder Rock

Robert Bolt
A Man for All Seasons
The Tiger and the
*   Horse*

Harold Brighouse
Hobson's Choice

Coxe and Chapman
Billy Budd

Gordon Daviot
Dickon

Barry England
Conduct Unbecoming

J. E. Flecker
Hassan

Ruth and Augustus
Goetz
The Heiress

H. Granville-Barker
The Voysey Inheritance

(Ed.) E. Haddon
Three Dramatic
*   Legends*

Willis Hall
The Long and the Short
*   and the Tall*

Fritz Hochwälder
The Strong are Lonely

Henrik Ibsen
The Master Builder
An Enemy of the People

D. H. Lawrence
The Widowing of Mrs
*   Holroyd and The*
*   Daughter-in-Law*

Roger MacDougall
Escapade

Arthur Miller
The Crucible
Death of a Salesman
All My Sons

André Obey
Noah

J. B. Priestley
An Inspector Calls
Time and the Conways
When We are Married

James Saunders
Next Time I'll Sing to
*   You*
A Scent of Flowers

R. C. Sherriff
Journey's End

J. M. Synge
The Playboy of the
*   Western World and*
*   Riders to the Sea*

Brandon Thomas
Charley's Aunt

Peter Ustinov
Romanoff and Juliet

John Whiting
Marching Song
Saint's Day
A Penny for a Song
The Devils

Oscar Wilde
The Importance of
*   Being Earnest*

Tennessee Williams
The Glass Menagerie

Peter Ustinov

Romanoff and Juliet

with an Introduction and Notes by
E. R. WOOD

HEINEMANN EDUCATIONAL BOOKS
LONDON

Heinemann Educational Books Ltd

LONDON   EDINBURGH   MELBOURNE   AUCKLAND   TORONTO
SINGAPORE   HONG KONG   KUALA LUMPUR
IBADAN   NAIROBI   JOHANNESBURG
NEW DELHI

ISBN 0 435 22913 3

Romanoff and Juliet © Peter Ustinov 1957
Introduction and Notes © E. R. Wood 1967
First published by the English Theatre Guild Ltd 1957
First published in the *Hereford Plays Series* 1967
Reprinted 1970, 1972

Published by
Heinemann Educational Books Ltd
48 Charles Street, London W1X 8AH
Printed and bound in Great Britain by
Morrison and Gibb Ltd
London and Edinburgh

16372 50

Contents

Introduction

PETER USTINOV was born in London in 1921 and educated at Westminster School and the London Theatre Studio. His father was a Russian, a press attaché at the German Embassy in London, who had married a French painter, Nadia Benon. On both sides he comes of interesting and artistic forebears, and he is married to the Canadian actress Suzanne Cloutier. 'I find relatives,' he says 'in every country I go to, so that I really feel perhaps more emotionally involved in the United Nations than in any individual country.' Some of the originality and ebullience of his mind may be attributed to his cosmopolitan origins.

He is well-known for memorable performances as an actor on stage and screen; he has written highly successful plays, novels and filmscripts; he has directed plays and films and produced opera at Covent Garden; on television he enjoys enviable gifts as a mimic and raconteur; he speaks six languages and can sing (for fun) all the parts in a Mozart opera. A critic has written of this man of multiple talents: 'He does admit humbly to having never worked with a circus or danced at Covent Garden – although one suspects that both institutions are the poorer for it.'

He wrote his first play, *House of Regrets*, at the age of 19. Among the best-known of its successors are *The Banbury Nose* (1943), *The Love of Four Colonels* (1951), *The Moment of Truth* (1951), *No Sign of the Dove* (1953), *Romanoff and Juliet* (1956) and *Photo Finish* (1963).

Romanoff and Juliet invites by its title comparison with Shakespeare's *Romeo and Juliet*. The situation is in essentials the same: we have a pair of 'star-crossed lovers' whose happiness is blighted by a bitter feud between their kinsfolk. Shakespeare's tragedy is wholly romantic: Ustinov's comedy is mainly ironic, and the irony is deepened by the echoes of Shakespeare. Even the setting of *Romanoff and Juliet* recalls Shakespeare's medieval Verona, but only to show how in the twentieth century the picturesque survivals are exploited by the tourist trade, and to suggest that the small city-state could exist in the modern power jungle only by the most intricate and cunning non-alignment policy. Resemblances between sets of lovers in the two plays only serve to emphasise differences in spirit. Igor Romanoff and Juliet Moulsworth are like Shakespeare's lovers in being helplessly swept along in the joyful-painful enchantment of love, but while Romeo and Juliet are wholly committed, without check of reason or doubt, their modern counterparts are conscious that the magic of the night does not stand up well to the cool reason of morning light. Romeo tells the priest about Juliet:

> Come what sorrow can
> It cannot countervail the exchange of joy
> That one short minute gives me in her sight,

and Juliet tells Romeo:

> All my fortunes at thy foot I'll lay,
> And follow thee, my lord, throughout the world.

Romanoff and his Juliet cannot maintain so exalted and emotional a pitch: their flights are subject to comic bumps caused by the deflating effect of daylight moods: 'Curious how romance tricks the otherwise logical mind into inaccuracies,' says Igor, when Juliet reminds him of what he had earlier said about being 'selflessly united in an endless waltz'. 'Naturally,' he goes on, 'the waltz could not have been endless, otherwise it would still be going on – and that is impossible since we are now here.'

Logic like this is the death of romance. So is arithmetical accuracy: Romeo might conceivably have asked his Juliet if she had ever kissed a man, but she could never have answered, as Juliet Moulsworth does, 'Only four. And Freddie.'

Despite numerous such lapses from the conversational level of high romance, we can believe in Igor and Juliet as a pair of lovers 'selflessly united'. The ironic contrast with the Shakespearean style is more striking when we consider Freddie and Junior Captain Marfa Zlotochienko. Their love scene is rich with the element of incongruity from which laughter springs.

In this play of many facets, the parallel with the most romantic of Shakespeare's tragedies is only one – comparatively minor – element. Much of the amusement comes from satire on Russian and American obsessions and idiosyncracies. Peter Ustinov's highly individual gifts and experience here bear delightful fruit. He has an accurate ear for oddities of speech and a mischievous eye for the ludicrous. Because he is free from national prejudices of his own and familiar with Russian and American life and behaviour, he is able to let his sense of fun play freely (and fairly impartially) over serious matters. The picture presented of opposed national and political attitudes, alike only in their solemnity and their craving for orthodoxy, is comically exaggerated but based on recognizable reality.

The characters in the Russian Embassy are all solemn, so that on one occasion when laughter *is* heard, the General says, 'What a curious noise!' In literature Russians do seem to be more introspective, more interested in agony and tears, than other peoples, so that we are not surprised when one character in *Romanoff and Juliet* says in bewilderment, 'Tell me, why am I not unhappy?' and another asks, 'How can one understand our great and tortured history except through the magnifying glass of tears?' In reality, of course, Russians are great laughers too, but there grew up after the Revolution a puritanical suspicion of fun and frivolity, and the typical communist of the Stalin era did not look much amused. People who are unable to laugh at themselves are particularly vulnerable to the satirist.

The play makes fun of the way in which the Communist mind could be stirred by allusions to the Revolutionary struggle. Hence the nostalgic references to the Winter Palace in Petrograd, whence the lights streamed from the windows on the peasants outside in the snow, or to messages being taken to the red sailors of the Baltic Fleet. At a later date good communists warmed to enthusiasm about statistics of the output of collective farms or tractor factories. There was an atmosphere in which an exclamation like 'Glory to our women trawler captains!' could be made without tongue in cheek, and insults like 'Trotskyist!' or 'Interventionist!' were rich with historical meaning. The 'pastimes' of criticism and confession were products of the regime of Stalin and his secret police. No doubt it was at first healthy that men in authority could be criticized, denounced and induced to admit their mistakes, but after the great purges of the 1930s, when heroes of the Civil War were 'liquidated' after making avowals of incredible sabotage and treachery, the subject was not funny. In *Romanoff and Juliet* Ustinov manages to treat it as a joke. The spy who is resident in the Russian Embassy, partly to serve as chauffeur, partly to report on his country's potential enemies, and partly to inform on his colleagues and superiors, is a comic figure. Marfa is rather more sinister; and it is to her that Romanoff recalls the hopes of the Revolution and shows how they have been betrayed:

> The machine-guns chattered in the cold, laughing victims fell painlessly to their death, the snow was stained with blood. Other voices took up the song, other feet stepped forward, other hands grasped home-made weapons. In the morning, victory was ours, and many of the dead were smiling still. Those were the days of our enthusiasm. And what has happened since? Our land has become a huge laboratory, a place of human test-tubes. Our language, so rich, so masculine, so muscular, is but a pale shadow of its possibilities. Our literature, which ravished the dark soul of man with such pity,

is now mobilised to serve an empty optimism. Our music, divorced from sadness and the twilight, has lost its anchor in an ocean of dreariness. You, my dear child, were born into this monotonous nursery, and you have never played with other toys than boredom, pride and smugness.

The passage is not to be taken too seriously; the mockery and burlesque are evident in the talk of home-made weapons and the smiling dead as well as in the nostalgia for sadness, but Ustinov is making a serious point, which George Orwell made more emphatically in *Animal Farm* and Arthur Koestler more grimly in *Darkness at Noon*. The ideals of the early days had come to seem too innocent.

If Peter Ustinov makes irreverent fun of serious aspects of Russian life a decade ago, he is no less mischievously satirical about the American way of life. The American male is shown to be limited in his interests, to money and sport; his ideas of international affairs are confined to a crude view of the Cold War as the struggle of Good against Evil. The American Ambassador is a caricature of the 'tough' American. He thinks he is a hard-headed realist. He can say to a young lover: 'Nowadays marriage like everything else is strictly business, and business is pressure. Go up there, son, and fight for your wife. Start shouting, or you'll lose her to the next customer.' But he is equally ludicrous in his sentimentality: 'I knew your father, son. He was a fine, upstanding man, and the best Number Three ever to row for Princeton.' Freddie is equally obsessed with sport. 'One thing about baseball,' he says. 'It never lets you down.' (Love, it seems, does.) When he has broken with Juliet, (because, like a good baseball player, he knows when he is licked) his tender farewell is in baseball terms: 'God bless you, baby. Keep pitching.'

Hooper and Freddie also lay themselves open to be laughed at because of their sententious platitudes. When Freddie, disappointed in his hopes of Juliet, sighs, 'I guess that's . . . life',

Hooper sighs too and adds, 'Never said a truer word, son. That's what it is, Life. The mighty Unpredictable.'

But Freddie, as a specimen of the comic American, familiar to us from the cinema world, is a joy to listen to. Though as undeveloped mentally and emotionally as the Ambassador, he is likeable and even touching in his awareness of his own inadequacy. 'It wouldn't have worked, kid,' he admits to Juliet; 'I don't talk good, but you know what I mean. There'd be days with my big corny smile and the way I talk; well, it'd only irritate you.'

In comedy, common sense is the touchstone by which folly is shown up. In this play the women have a little more of it than the men (assuming that we can regard Junior Captain Zlotchienko as more like a man than a woman). They show it in their attitude to the Feud. The Cold War was a grimmer obsession a decade ago (when the play was written) than it is today. The women in *Romanoff and Juliet* are more ready to break free of it than the men. It is a very serious matter to the American Ambassador. When he realizes that his daughter is in love with a Communist he says, 'It may be she could be guilty of attempting to destroy the government of the United States by force . . . It may sound ridiculous to you and to me, but it won't sound so ridiculous before a Federal Investigating Committee.' He is hardly exaggerating. In the days of Senator McCarthy's Unamerican Activities Committee an association with a Communist could indeed lead to 'indictment and ruin'. On the Russian side suspicion of Western capitalism and scorn of Western decadence were at least as bitter.

The Cold War could be held to justify extreme developments in the nonsense of Espionage. The author makes farcical fun of this human activity, pushing it to its final logic when the General passes from one side to the other the latest complications resulting from knowledge of each others' code. His final report, 'They know you know they know you know the code', is a hilarious take-off of the grim world of spying described by such authors as John le Carré.

The third party in the power struggle is the Smallest Country in Europe, which is rather more than a Twentieth Century version of Shakespeare's Verona. It has some of the picturesque quaintness of a tiny independent state like Liechtenstein or Andorra, together with the political shrewdness of Vienna or Berne. Its president is entirely cynical about military alliances. 'We tactfully declared war on Germany,' he says, 'several hours before her surrender. As a consequence we were offered six acres of land which didn't belong to us by the grateful Allies. This we cleverly refused. And now we are on good terms with everybody.' As for military glory, he has no illusions. 'At the age of four with paper hats and wooden swords,' he declares, 'we're all generals. Only some of us never grow out of it.' This tiny fairy-tale state, it seems, has only two soldiers. We have no cannons,' the General explains; 'we need no fodder.' But his views on the war game are not frivolous: he sees politics, war and the predicament of his country with cool realism. There is a fine bitter passage on night and day in which he speaks of dawn:

How I hate the dawn! It's the hour of the firing squad. The last glass of brandy. The ultimate cigarette. The final wish. All the hideously calculated hypocrisy of men when they commit a murder in the name of justice. Then it's the time of Death on a grander scale, the hour of the great offensives . . . fix your bayonets, boys . . . Gentlemen, synchronize your watches . . . in ten seconds' time the barrage starts . . . a thousand men are destined to die in order to capture a farmhouse no one has lived in for years . . . And finally, dawn is the herald of the day, our twelve hours of unimportance, when we have to cede to the pressures of the powers, smile at people we have every reason but expediency to detest . . .

Although the General is involved in several comic scenes, nobody makes a fool of him. He is shrewder than either of the ambassadors (he has to be to survive) and he disarms ridicule by self-mockery. Moreover, the General is a skilful manipulator, who finally manages like a benevolent uncle to make all end well.

The foregoing analysis of the satirical element in *Romanoff and Juliet* perhaps over-emphasizes its serious basis; for the general spirit of the play is that of light-hearted fantasy with a touch of melancholy. It is set in a dream-city – 'the dream which every tortured modern man may carry in his sleep'. Like Shakespeare's Illyria or the Forest of Arden, it is a place where things come right in the end. The atmosphere is not at all realistic. It would not be difficult to imagine *Romanoff and Juliet* adapted to make a ballet or a musical. It is an entertainment which consciously uses the varied resources of the stage. Soon after his first appearance the General steps out of the play to address the audience directly, rather like a character from Thornton Wilder or Brecht. Later he sings a mock-sentimental, mock-patriotic song, in which the two soldiers join. Nobody actually does a dance, but the movements have some of the formality of ballet. The artifice of the staging, with the front walls of the opposed embassies flown in turn for the playing of alternating interior scenes, and the clock with its wobbling figure of Death the Reaper, all suggest a performance as overtly theatrical as a puppet show. The balancing of some of the scenes in the two embassies, and the movement of the General from one to the other, prepare us for the charade of the wedding scene, where the mock-ritual is intoned and interwoven with interruptions in the style of comic opera. The design is completed when the General again addresses the audience, and the two soldiers are left playing the game with which they opened the play.

The language too is elegant rather than naturalistic. There is a good deal of paradox which recalls Shaw or Wilde. 'I met your mother for the first time at our wedding,' says the elder Romanoff. 'There was not time for surprise. We were both spared the degradation of emotional behaviour.' The spy says sadly, 'To me women surrender everything but their secrets, and their company makes me feel more lonely than I feel alone.' Some of the satirical shafts at the communists have a paradoxical point. There is the communist idea of Democracy: 'With the advent of Democracy, we are now given the choice of belief or disbelief, but naturally we are put on our honour to make the right choice. Otherwise Democracy would have no meaning.' There is a special interpretation of Freedom: 'This is a free country. We have a right to share your privacy in a public place.' Similarly paradox is behind some of the jokes about American ideals: 'He was of the let-the-best-man-win school. He always won. He weighed 'most three hundred pounds.' (Beulah's comment is 'Women just adore brave men!'). Hooper says about the need for Beauty in life: 'I like Beauty when it's practical, Beulah,' and about Freddie being sensitive: 'A little mousy guy I can understand being sensitive, but a guy his size just hasn't the right.' The quality of paradox depends on the amount of truth that emerges from saying the opposite of what is expected. An example of this is found when the General recognises love in two young people, and remarks, 'I can see from your utter misery, from your eagerness to misunderstand each other, and from your thoroughly bad temper, that this is the real thing.'

Ustinov is fond of the reply which is funny in what is implied rather than what is said. For example, when Juliet asks Igor, 'Have you known many women?' he answers, 'I am a sailor by profession.'

When the situation calls for romantic eloquence, the language is pushed to the edge of extravagance and then over it into mockery. Igor exults poetically about being in love, and goes on to talk of the silences: 'Silences that seem to wander among the stars . . . the tender gravity of our silences' and then goes on, 'Oh, how undignified to feel the hot tears rolling down where rain and sleet hammer so ineffectually! Remember in your lucid moments, Igor Vadimovitch Romanoff, that you are second in command of a warship. ...' Even the General's concluding speech, full of soothing charm, ends in a joke.

Romanoff and Juliet is a play of sunshine and shadow, and while we are laughing at the fun we should be aware of a wry seriousness. The following quotation from a magazine article is relevant: 'Making people laugh is, for me, another way of being serious ... Tragedy is always painful, and it is through Comedy that I seem to express myself, so as not to transmit even a fraction of my own sadness.' The writer is Peter Ustinov.

AUTHOR'S NOTE

In the original production, the two Embassies were constructed on trucks which were fixed to the stage at one point, so that the entire buildings could be pivoted on stage and off easily and at will. This scheme proved eminently satisfactory, as it enlarged the acting area considerably when the interiors of the Embassies were not in use. It also enabled the General to seem to push the Embassies out of his mind at the end of the second act, when, at the climax of his Herculean labour in the devious world of diplomacy, he discovers that at last he has told the American Ambassador a piece of news which the latter had not yet gleaned from tapped wire or grapevine. This careless gesture of apparently Samsonesque strength added to the meaning of the play by its simple symbolism.

The crowd effects, fireworks, and musical numbers in the third act were, on the whole, left out in the London production, but have been left in the script to give the reader an impression of what was in the author's mind before the realities of a theatrical budget cast their shadow over his hopes. In fact, some of these diversions might only have confused the issue, and the play is a perfectly practical proposition without them.

November, 1956

CHARACTERS

FIRST SOLDIER
SECOND SOLDIER
THE GENERAL
HOOPER MOULSWORTH
VADIM ROMANOFF
IGOR ROMANOFF
JULIET MOULSWORTH
THE SPY
BEULAH MOULSWORTH
EVDOKIA ROMANOFF
JUNIOR CAPTAIN MARFA ZLOTOCHIENKO
FREDDIE VANDERSTUYT
THE ARCHBISHOP

ACT ONE: Dawn to Morning.
ACT TWO: Noon to Afternoon.
ACT THREE: Evening to Night.

The Main Square in the Capital City of the Smallest
Country in Europe.

Romanoff and Juliet was presented by Linnit and Dunfee Ltd at the Piccadilly Theatre on 17 May 1956, with the following cast:

FIRST SOLDIER	*Joe Gibbons*
SECOND SOLDIER	*David Lodge*
THE GENERAL	*Peter Ustinov*
HOOPER MOULSWORTH	*John Phillips*
VADIM ROMANOFF	*Frederick Valk*
IGOR ROMANOFF	*Michael David*
JULIET MOULSWORTH	*Katy Vail*
THE SPY	*David Hurst*
BEULAH MOULSWORTH	*Josephine Barrington*
EVDOKIA ROMANOFF	*Marianne Deeming*
JUNIOR CAPTAIN MARFA ZLOTOCHIENKO	
	Delphi Lawrence
FREDDIE VANDERSTUYT	*William Greene*
THE ARCHBISHOP	*Edward Atienza*

The Play directed by
DENIS CAREY

ACT ONE

Dawn to morning,
The Main Square in the Capital City of the Smallest Country in
Europe. It is dawn. Sombre building on the left with a balcony.
Sombre building on the right with balcony. In the background, a
cathedral, with an illuminated clock, on which a great many
unsteady saints frequently appear together with Father Time,
Death the Reaper, and other allegorical figures, to hammer out
fractions of the hour. The sky is expansive, and has the crystal-
line purity of early dawn in the south. SOLDIER *left.* SOLDIER *right.*
Both in the shadows.

FIRST SOLDIER: Your turn to start.
SECOND SOLDIER: T.
FIRST SOLDIER: R.
SECOND SOLDIER: T.R . . . A.
FIRST SOLDIER: N.
SECOND SOLDIER: T.R.A.N . . . S.
FIRST SOLDIER: U.
SECOND SOLDIER: U? No such word.
FIRST SOLDIER: Yes, there is.
SECOND SOLDIER: Well, if there is, it's not spelled that way.
FIRST SOLDIER: Yes, it is.
SECOND SOLDIER: Ah!
FIRST SOLDIER: Ah . . .
SECOND SOLDIER: T.R.A.N.S.U.B.
FIRST SOLDIER: S.
SECOND SOLDIER: T.
FIRST SOLDIER: A.
SECOND SOLDIER: N.
FIRST SOLDIER: T.

SECOND SOLDIER: I.

FIRST SOLDIER: A.

SECOND SOLDIER: T.

FIRST SOLDIER: I. Oh, damn.

SECOND SOLDIER: You should have foreseen that O. (*Long pause.*) I said O.

FIRST SOLDIER: I still don't think it's spelled that way.

SECOND SOLDIER: Go on. Say it. N.

FIRST SOLDIER: Transubstantiation? I'm sure it's got three esses somewhere.

SECOND SOLDIER: I gave you Rhododendron just now, although I'm damn sure there's only one H in it.

FIRST SOLDIER: All right, all right. What's that make the score?

SECOND SOLDIER (*consulting a bit of paper awkwardly in the dark*): Eight twenty-four to seven sixty-seven.

FIRST SOLDIER: Who's eight hundred and twenty-four?

SECOND SOLDIER: I am.

FIRST SOLDIER: Bastard.

SECOND SOLDIER: Well, I was eight twenty-three before. Stands to reason.

FIRST SOLDIER: I won't argue. It only goes to show that the night's too long.

SECOND SOLDIER: It's nearly over. (*He consults his watch.*) Death's late.

FIRST SOLDIER: Death? They don't know how to oil him properly.

SECOND SOLDIER: Your turn to start.

FIRST SOLDIER: Oh, hell. Z.

SECOND SOLDIER: That's easy. E.

FIRST SOLDIER: I suppose you're thinking of Zebra?

SECOND SOLDIER: How did you guess?

FIRST SOLDIER: Well—A.

SECOND SOLDIER: What? A? Nonsense. Oh——

FIRST SOLDIER: Ah.

SECOND SOLDIER (*mumming*): Zeaa, Zeab, Zeac, Zead, Zeae,
Zeaf, Zeag.

FIRST SOLDIER (*cruelly*): Take your time.

A FIGURE *appears in the uniform of an operetta general, sky blue
and silver. He wears a carnival mask round his neck.*

SECOND SOLDIER: Zeah, Zeai, Zeaf. Cave. A General.

GENERAL: Take your time. Finish your game.

SECOND SOLDIER: I give up. L. What's that?

FIRST SOLDIER (*leering*): Eight twenty-four to seven sixty-
eight. Now, where's my bloody rifle? It was here a moment
ago.

SECOND SOLDIER: My turn to give the order.

FIRST SOLDIER: O.K., but hang on, let me find the—where
the hell is it?

GENERAL: Getting warmer . . . warmer . . .

The rifle drops with a clatter as the SOLDIER *walks into it.*

Ah !

FIRST SOLDIER: Got it. Fire ahead.

SECOND SOLDIER (*colloquial*): Regiment. Regiment, pre-sent
—are you ready?

FIRST SOLDIER: Yes, only hurry, it's heavy.

SECOND SOLDIER: Pre-sent—ahms !

They do so, with insulting untidiness, in their own time.

GENERAL (*saluting*): Thank you very much. That was a kind
thought.

FIRST SOLDIER: Don't mention it.

GENERAL (*takes out a heavy gold watch*): Any sign of Death yet?

SECOND SOLDIER: No, sir.

GENERAL: I make him ten minutes late.

There's a strange sound of creaking machinery.

Listen !

*They all look at the clock. The wobbling figure of Death the
Reaper emerges, and hits a bell with sickening force. The
sound produced, however, is dull and unresonant.*

FIRST SOLDIER: He's getting old.

GENERAL (*shrugging*): Fourteenth century. Hardly adolescent by our standards.

FIRST SOLDIER (*bitterly*): Our standards.

GENERAL (*reasonably*): You must be a Socialist, young man.

FIRST SOLDIER: Socialist Agrarian Reform Peasants' Industrial Party.

GENERAL: I've never heard of it.

FIRST SOLDIER: I'm a founder member.

GENERAL: Do you vote?

FIRST SOLDIER: Nearly every day.

GENERAL: That's what I like to hear. A true democrat.

FIRST SOLDIER: We get time off to vote.

GENERAL: Yes, yes, of course. So do I.

SECOND SOLDIER: I don't hold with his views, General.

GENERAL: Oh, perhaps you belong to my party?

SECOND SOLDIER: The National Iron Fist. The Nif. (*He salutes strangely.*) We wear orange shirts . . . or we would do if we could afford them.

GENERAL: No, I'm afraid I don't know that either. I'm Rally of Unionist Separist Extremes, sometimes known as the R.U.S.E. Anyone——?

FIRST SOLDIER
SECOND SOLDIER } No, Sorry. . . .

GENERAL: How strange. It's the party at present in power.

FIRST SOLDIER: There hasn't been a party in power since the ultimate dictatorship of last year's season.

GENERAL: I stand corrected. Of course, you are quite right. We govern by coalitions. What I meant to say is that we hold the casting vote in the present coalition. In fact, I am President of the Republic.

SECOND SOLDIER: At the moment?

GENERAL: Yes. I have been for some ten hours.

FIRST SOLDIER: You're doing well. (*Extends his right hand.*)

GENERAL: May I? (*Shakes First Soldier's hand.*) Thank you very much. (*With a sigh.*) Yes. We judge a dog's life as being roughly one-seventh that of a man. But a president doesn't even deserve a dog's life. His expectancy is roughly one-seventh that of a mayfly. (*He suddenly looks at the audience and smiles.*) Look at us——

FIRST SOLDIER } (*challenging the audience as they see it for*
SECOND SOLDIER } *the first time*): Halt! Who goes there?

GENERAL: Put your rifles away.

SECOND SOLDIER: It may be wiser. We're outnumbered.

FIRST SOLDIER: Are those people out there in the shadows?

GENERAL: Yes, and we must be very polite to them; we're entirely dependent on our tourist trade. (*He addresses the audience*). Good evening. You will find us only on the very best atlases, because we are the smallest country left in Europe—and when I say country, I don't mean principality or grand duchy. I don't mean a haven for gambling or income tax evasion—I mean self-respecting country which deserves, and sometimes achieves, a colour of its own on the map—usually a dyspeptic mint green, which misses the outline of the frontier by a fraction of an inch, so that one can almost hear the printer saying damn. Our population is so small, that it's not worth counting. We have no cannons, we need no fodder. (*To Second Soldier.*) Don't fiddle with your rifle, there's a sport. It's dangerous.

SECOND SOLDIER: They're only blanks.

GENERAL (*shocked*): I should hope so!

SECOND SOLDIER: Well, I believe in armed force.

GENERAL: Oh, on statues, symbolized by a cluster of angels striding upwards into nowhere, there's nothing like it.

SECOND SOLDIER: Do you mean that, as a general, you're not the tiniest bit ambitious for our military future?

GENERAL: I prefer our military past. The harm's done and there it is. As for being a general, well at the age of four with paper hats and wooden swords we're all generals. Only some of us never grow out of it.

SECOND SOLDIER: But—aren't you proud of the fact that we won the last war?

FIRST SOLDIER: No one won the last war.

GENERAL: We tactfully declared war on Germany several hours before her surrender. As a consequence we were offered six acres of land which didn't belong to us by the grateful Allies. This we cleverly refused. And now we are on good terms with everyone.

FIRST SOLDIER: You live in the past, General. Our future lies in the abolition of frontiers. The day will dawn when the workers will tear down the Customs sheds, demolish the road blocks, and extend the hand of friendship across the artificial gulfs imposed by nationalists and capitalist warmongers.

GENERAL (sadly): You read a great deal, don't you?

SECOND SOLDIER: Our future lies in our discipline and in the cultivation of heroism in the very young. To my mind, every mother who has successfully borne five children should be given a free issue of toy bayonets by a grateful nation.

GENERAL: And yet, my dear friends, our love for what is ours is far subtler, far deeper than all your silly foreign ideas. And I'll prove it to you. I only have to start singing a folk-song for you two to join in, despite your better judgement.

FIRST SOLDIER ⎫
SECOND SOLDIER ⎬ (derisively): Folk-song!

GENERAL (singing softly, and with love):
>An angel weary of Paradise
>Came down to visit the Earth.
>She floated over hill and dale
>Till she heard laughter and mirth.
>
>What is that ripple of happiness
>That wafts through the trees like a song?
>What is that shout of banners
>Which crowns the distant throng?

It's our army of rocking horses
Off to a bloodless war.
It's our princes and captains
On their way to the sandy shore.

Our swords are made of good white wood.
Our castles are made of sand,
Our lances are made of plasticine;
We're off to defend our land!

The angel returned to Paradise
A younger, wiser girl,
And swore she'd never journey again
Her head was in a whirl.

For as the sky has its paradise
So the Earth has its pearl;
Our country! Our country!
The Earth has its pearl!

Gradually the other two have joined in, at first humming the melody, then singing elaborately and fluently in parts. They finish. A silence.

SECOND SOLDIER: Well, we did it.

FIRST SOLDIER (*disgusted*): And to think the words are meaningless. They're nursery rhyme stuff, devoid of a social message.

GENERAL (*serenely*): Social messages change according to social conditions, while nursery rhyme nonsense is eternal. It has set many a wise foot tapping, and has cradled the great men and the idiots of tomorrow in a lilting sleep.

A window of the building on the audience's right opens with a clatter. An angry man in pyjamas, and wearing rimless glasses, looks out.

ANGRY MAN: Can't a guy get a decent night's rest round here? If it is not the cathedral clock, it's drunks.

GENERAL: Drunks? I beg your pardon, Ambassador.

ANGRY MAN: Who's that? Oh, Mr President—please forgive my outburst. It was a great party last night. Or should I say this morning.

GENERAL: Thank you.

ANGRY MAN: The idea of wearing masks was just great.

GENERAL (*modest*): It's traditional.

ANGRY MAN: Hey? I still have mine on! What do you know? The damnedest thing! (*And indeed a black mask, adorns his forehead like the goggles of a motor-cyclist.*) Well, sure makes me wish you had Independence Day every day.

GENERAL: We do, but we can't afford to celebrate it more than ten or fifteen times a year.

ANGRY MAN: Is that so?

GENERAL: We have gained our independence at least four hundred times, which makes us cumulatively the most independent people in Europe.

ANGRY MAN: Is that so? Well, that's certainly worth knowing.

GENERAL: Unfortunately, we have lost our independence even more frequently.

ANGRY MAN: Is that a fact? You sure live and learn.

WOMAN (*voice, hooting*): Hooper!

ANGRY MAN: Coming, sugar.

WOMAN (*voice*): Are you crazy, standing in that window with your arthritis?

ANGRY MAN (*sheepish*): Well, I guess you fellers heard. See you. (*He disappears.*)

FIRST SOLDIER (*sour*): Warmonger!

The opposite window opens, and another angry man looks out.

SECOND ANGRY MAN: Ppsst!

GENERAL: Ambassador! Good morning.

SECOND ANGRY MAN: He said something?

GENERAL: Who?

SECOND ANGRY MAN: Him. He——

GENERAL: Not much, no.

SECOND ANGRY MAN: I can hear him speak if I put my ear to the window, but I can only catch the sounds, not the words.

GENERAL: We woke him up with our singing. I hope we didn't do the same to you.

SECOND ANGRY MAN: I don't sleep.

GENERAL: Never?

SECOND ANGRY MAN: Never.

GENERAL: Insomnia?

SECOND ANGRY MAN: Policy.

GENERAL: Gracious.

SECOND ANGRY MAN: May I congratulate you, Mr President, on the reception last night, which perceptibly increased our solidarity?

GENERAL: I enjoyed it. I was the last to leave, and got rather drunk.

SECOND ANGRY MAN (*without humour*): Drunkenness in pursuit of solidarity is not a sin.

WOMAN (*voice, strident*): Vadim!

SECOND ANGRY MAN: Da, golubchik.

WOMAN (*voice*): Paidi Suda!

SECOND ANGRY MAN (*conciliatory*): Sichas . . .

GENERAL: You'd better go.

SECOND ANGRY MAN (*suspicious*): You understand our language?

GENERAL: I understand . . . the situation.

Abruptly the SECOND ANGRY MAN *disappears. A decrepit saint strikes the bell.*

St Simeon Stylites . . . I make it seven sixteen.

FIRST SOLDIER: Seven four.

SECOND SOLDIER: A quarter to eight.

They put their watches away.

GENERAL: Oh, well, St Simeon never had much use for time, up there on his giddy column.

FIRST SOLDIER: That clock's a national disgrace.

SECOND SOLDIER: For once I agree with you.

GENERAL: Why? The only one who's always punctual is Death
... whatever the time, he always strikes his knell at the first
streak of dawn ... and believe me, he knows what he's doing.
How I hate the dawn! It's the hour of the firing squad. The
last glass of brandy. The ultimate cigarette. The final wish.
All the hideously calculated hypocrisy of men when they
commit a murder in the name of justice. Then it's the time of
Death on a grander scale, the hour of the great offensives ...
fix your bayonets, boys. .... Gentlemen, synchronize your
watches ... in ten seconds' time the barrage starts ... a
thousand men are destined to die in order to capture a farmhouse no one has lived in for years. .... And finally, dawn is
the herald of the day, our twelve hours of unimportance,
when we have to cede to the pressures of the powers, smile
at people we have every reason but expediency to detest.
... A diplomat these days is nothing but a head-waiter who's
allowed to sit down occasionally. .... (*Playing to the house on
audience's left.*) Yes, sir, and how do you want your imports,
in oil? In petrol! Underdone? Overdone? If I may say so, sir,
your taste is impeccable. May I say so, sir? Thank you very
much. (*Playing to the house on audience's right.*) Yes, sir, of
course, I guarantee not to serve the other customer any
secrets. .... I'll tell him secrets are off the menu—although
you and I know, don't we, sir, that—? Ha, ha, ha—(*Surprised*). Sir, service is included. .... Oh, well ... if you insist.
... (*With elaborate gratitude.*) Thank *you very* much. .... (*He
comes up from his deep reverence and looks searchingly at the
soldiers.*) You hate the night because you find it boring. ....
I hate the day because it's an insult to my intelligence, a slur
on my honour, and a worm in the heart of my integrity,
whereas the night ... (*He basks in his thought.*) ... That night
is marvellous ... because it is the time when the great
powers are asleep, recovering their energies for the horrors
of the ensuing day ... and in that time of magic and of
mystery, our horizons are infinite ... they stretch not only

to the north, south, east, and west, but up towards the moon, down towards the centre of the earth. In peace, and in harmony with nature, we send out our vast battalions to colonize the imagination. . . . When others sleep, our Empire knows no bounds.

A cock crows. The street lamps go out.

(*Heavily.*) There. Our daily winter has begun.

SECOND SOLDIER (*softly*): Look.

GENERAL: Oh, look.

A pair of lovers wander into the square, too involved in each other to know where they are. They wear evening dress, and masks dangle round their necks.

(*Softly, heartfelt.*) Oh, I hope they found each other very early in the night, for now he may notice a wrinkle under the weary, longing eye, while she may spy a trace of cruel satisfaction around his mouth. (*Sadly*). Ah, the morning after! Ah, dawn! Let us be tactful.

FIRST SOLDIER: My turn to give the order.

GENERAL: Sh! Dismiss, but for goodness sake don't do it as you were taught.

FIRST SOLDIER (*whispering*): Regiment. Salute the flag! Dismiss!

They march off on tiptoe with a last sentimental look at the lovers. The lovers break from a long, long kiss and look at each other in adoration.

HE: Are there words which have not been used before?

SHE: There are silences which have not been shared before. Why do you look at me so critically?

HE: Critically?

SHE: Are there bags under my eyes?

HE: I would be lying if I told you you weren't tired.

SHE (*hiding her face*): Then don't look at me.

HE (*lifting her face again*): I want to guess what you will look like at seventy.

SHE: It's late. We're getting silly. It's the sunlight and the weariness and the sad farewell of old champagne on the tongue. There was no edge to our thoughts when the candles and the cut-glass ornaments sent shivering milky-ways up to the ceiling, and when your eyes sparkled like mineral wealth from the rock of your face.

HE (*sadly*): You can't recapture it by language.

SHE: I know.

HE: Enchantment fades so quickly that after five minutes you doubt if it was ever there.

SHE: Do you doubt it?

HE: No. I remember it.

SHE (*desperate*): But I am still here!

HE (*holding her*): Yes, a warm, a living thing, which I desire. Last night we were as one, creatures in a dream, selflessly united in an endless waltz. From now on we are opposed, a man and a woman in love—the greatest, most exhausting struggle in the world—two moths racing for the flame, two cannibals devouring each other.

SHE: Have you known many women?

HE: I am a sailor by profession.

SHE: Thank you for your honesty.

HE (*smiles*): You're afraid that I will compare you to the others?

SHE: Inevitably.

HE: And what if I say that you are better?

SHE: That's not enough. I want to be alone.

HE: You have never kissed a man?

SHE: Only four. And Freddie.

HE: Do you mean only four, and Freddie? Or do you mean five?

SHE (*surprised, she turns it over in her mind*): Five? No, I mean four, and Freddie.

HE: Who's Freddie?

SHE (*enraptured*): You're jealous!

HE: I'm waiting for an answer.

SHE: Freddie? He's my fiancé.

HE: I see.

SHE (*a little foolishly*): He's in refrigerators.

HE: I don't understand.

SHE: He makes refrigerators. His father made refrigerators before him.

HE: A hereditary gift.

SHE: Freddie believes he has a mission in refrigeration. He told me once when he was drunk that in the event of war, he has a device which can freeze the Gulf Stream, and make everyone but us very uncomfortable. Oh, Lord, I shouldn't be telling you this, should I?

HE: No.

SHE: You have no accent, darling. I keep forgetting who you are.

HE (*with pomp*): I serve aboard the icebreaker *Red October*. Ironic, isn't it, that it may one day be my duty to crash through Freddie's most cherished daydream.

SHE: Oh, how awful. Now everything's spoiled.

HE (*kindly*): Why? Surely love recognizes no didactic frontiers?

SHE (*desperate*): But Igor! Creatures in a dream, selflessly united in an endless waltz—

HE: I said that, didn't I?

SHE: Yes.

HE: Curious how romance tricks the otherwise logical mind into inaccuracies. Naturally, the waltz could not have been endless, otherwise it would still be going on—(*As he sees her incredulous face*)—and that is impossible since we are now here.

SHE (*in real agony*): Oh, no!

HE (*suddenly*): Does what I say sound very humourless and . . . and un-Western when I talk like that? (*Silence.*) I must apologize. I can never regret a phenomenon as beautiful or as powerful as our love, but I must admit that it has created within me the most reprehensible ideological confusion. I must consult my textbooks before I can hope to interpret to you in scientific terms the exact extent of my spiritual deviation.

SHE (*hopefully*): You mean you love me more than Marx?

HE (*sharply*): Please do not speak sarcastically. It doesn't suit you.

SHE: I'm sorry, but I'm jealous of the man.

HE: I do not make light of your beliefs.

SHE (*tenderly*): I can't make you out.

HE (*running his hands through his hair in agony*): I can't make myself out. It's all so simple in the Arctic.

SHE: Do you blame the climate, my darling?

HE: No. No, it's relatively simple in the Black Sea also.

SHE: You blame the dry land then?

HE: Yes. It must be that. Although a great deal of good solid work has been accomplished on dry land. That is undeniable. In fact, a considerable amount of *Das Kapital* was conceived in the British Museum, which makes it all the more remarkable.

SHE: Women? In general. Do they confuse you, dearest?

HE: Women? I've seen women before. I served on a ship under a woman captain, although in fairness to her, you wouldn't have guessed that she was a woman. *She* did not disturb me in the least. (*Slowly, and with considerable difficulty.*) The fact is, I love you.

SHE (*ecstatic*): Oh . . .

HE (*severe*): Please don't interrupt me. For my own good, for our future, I must analyse my reasons for loving you in spite of vast and irreconcilable spiritual and political divergencies. First of all, we were wearing masks. Your mask could have hidden the eager face of a freckled collective-farm girl. When we tore them off at midnight, it was already too late. I was in love.

SHE: Oh, Igor, that's not true. No collective-farm girl has an American accent.

HE: Yes, I was cheating. Forgive me. (*Fierce.*) I must be honest with myself. I think I know what drew me irresistibly towards you.

SHE (*coquettish*): What is it?

HE (*very serious*): You couldn't possibly be the captain of a ship. You're one of the only women I've ever met who couldn't possibly be the captain of a ship.

SHE: Dad bought me a dinghy last fall. It's moored near Cape Cod. I love the sea, angel, just the way you do.

HE (*gentle*): Could you bring a six-thousand-ton cargo ship into Murmansk harbour . . . without a pilot . . . backwards . . . in a snow storm?

SHE: I've never tried.

HE: No, you couldn't. And nor could I. Glory to our women trawler-captains.

SHE: Glory to them indeed. Kiss me.

HE: Not yet. I must first reach certain ethical conclusions.

SHE: Igor, there's so little time! (*To break his mood.*) I know what I like about you.

HE: What?

SHE: Your profile.

HE: The façade.

SHE: I never read a book unless I like the title. Igor, I like the title. I want to read the book.

HE: I fail to understand.

SHE: I like that, too. You could never understand. Kiss me.

HE: I forbid——

SHE: You want to.

HE: No.

SHE: Please!

HE: Thank you.

> *They embrace, and lose themselves in the silent game of love, oblivious to all around them. The* TWO SOLDIERS *reappear, one from either side, now dressed as peasants, in rags. Both carry various merchandize. They see each other with some annoyance.*

FIRST SOLDIER: Aren't you resting?

SECOND SOLDIER: It's too hot to sleep.

FIRST SOLDIER: It didn't take you long to change into your
street clothes.

SECOND SOLDIER: The same might be said of you. I believe
you tried to cash in on the market before I was properly up
and about. Not a very socialistic impulse, if I may say so.
(*Suddenly, cooing to the lovers.*) Keepsakes, bangles, prehistoric
coins, religious postcards beautifully picked out in silk and
sequins.

FIRST SOLDIER (*angry*): You jumped the gun! (*Glutinous.*)
Peanuts, traditional salted marzipan, raffia table-runners,
English collar studs, back numbers of *True Detective
Magazine*.

SECOND SOLDIER: There's nothing more suitable to announce
your engagement to your friends than a nice religious
postcard. It takes away all frivolous aspects from the negotiation, and has a spontaneous dignity which no amount of
subsequent teasing can ever dispel. On the other hand, if the
minor prophets picked out in petit-point seem too formal
for the younger approach, shall we say, I have a large
selection of cards which fall into the profane to saucy
category—milady surprised in her bath, in art colours that
will not run—Cupid's indiscretions, a lovely series in a new
Japanese polychrome process, smuggled into the country
only last Wednesday——

FIRST SOLDIER: No table is complete without raffia table-
runners and, incidentally, I can supply the table as well. The
clash of raffia and mahogany may seem abrupt, and even
startling, to the eye as yet unattuned to artistic adventure——

HE: Yes, but——

FIRST SOLDIER: —Yet I am assured that even Paris, that
mecca of the beau-monde, is following, albeit timidly, the
trail we so boldly blazed. No? Now, my friends, let us not be
blind idealists—love's first impulse quickly deepens into
habit—a habit which is termed a 'mature understanding between two people'. It is at this second, and far more im-

portant, stage of marriage that these complete back numbers of *True Detective* will come in more than handy. Husband back home late, madam? Baby crying, sir? Here is a nerve-steadying remedy—tales of horror and revenge, at a quarter of their original price!

SHE (*desperate*): Oh, do please leave us alone!

SECOND SOLDIER: This is a free country, madam. We have a right to share your privacy in a public place.

The lovers resume their interrupted kiss. The GENERAL *enters in a morning suit.*

GENERAL: What? Still at it? This must be what they call the real thing.

FIRST SOLDIER: It must be! Death to commerce.

GENERAL: The real thing! And I don't even know the false thing! You live, and learn that you know nothing.

SHE (*spinning round, furious*): Oh, please——!

GENERAL (*amazed; adjusting his pince-nez*): Miss Moulsworth!

SHE: Sh! Don't tell Dad, please!

GENERAL: I envied your idyll without ever realizing it involved the much-admired Miss Juliet. Merciful heavens, Lieutenant Romanoff!

HE: Silence! (*He looks round nervously.*) I implore you not to say a word of this to anyone. If you do, my career is finished.

The GENERAL *laughs.*

HE: Why do you laugh?

GENERAL: I began life as a ne'er-do-well, but was discovered cheating at cards, and so my career was finished. Look at me now.

HE: You are confusing me.

SHE: Oh, please, don't confuse him!

GENERAL: Are you really in love? I ask as an innocent, not as a technician.

SHE: Yes, only he won't let himself go. It's psychological. He's gotten to the stage of sorting out his emotions, and kind of freeing them from all those men, you know, Marx, Lenin, Trotsky.

HE (*rising, violent*): Trotsky! I can never forgive you for that!

GENERAL (*hastily*): She meant Engels. The names are somewhat similar. You need my help.

HE: No.

GENERAL: Yes, I can see from your utter misery, from your eagerness to misunderstand each other, and from your thoroughly bad temper, that this is the real thing. You wish to meet again tonight?

HE ⎫
SHE ⎭ No.

GENERAL: Yes, very well, I'll see what I can do. Tonight is the thousandth anniversary of our liberation from the Lithuanians.

FIRST SOLDIER: Is it really? I thought——

GENERAL: Who cares for accuracy? It may not have been a thousand years ago, and it almost certainly wasn't the Lithuanians, but we celebrate whatever it was tonight, and that's an order.

SECOND SOLDIER: With fireworks?

GENERAL: Naturally. With whatever we can afford. (*The* SECOND SOLDIER *produces a couple of rockets from his pocket to the disgust of the First Soldier.*) Two fireworks. Well done. It will be dark at eight o'clock.

GENERAL: Leave it to me.

HE ⎫
SHE ⎭ No!

GENERAL: Does eight o'clock seem very long to wait? I understand: Try not to be impatient.

HE (*abruptly*): Goodbye.

GENERAL: That's right. This is no time for emotion. Bear your separation with fortitude.

SHE: I'm going.

GENERAL: That's it. Bite your lip, like a heroine.

Without looking round, the lovers go to their respective Embassies. They are tempted to look back at the door.

No, no, resist temptation! Orpheus, don't look back at Eurydice! There are only twelve hours of Hades. Earn your joy tonight!

Precipitately, the lovers disappear. The GENERAL *sighs romantically; the* SOLDIERS *dry their eyes.*

We're a sentimental people . . .

FIRST SOLDIER: I'm glad I didn't sell any of those stinking table-runners . . . they deserve better . . .

SECOND SOLDIER: And my postcards are in such bad taste . . .

GENERAL: Oh, my God! (*With sudden anguish.*) I thought of it as a love story, beautiful, pure, simple. Simple? . . . . it's a diplomatic earthquake!

As he freezes, a MAN *dressed as a spy enters, looking too anonymous to be possible. He goes quickly and silently to the Second Soldier.*

SPY: Have they arrived?

SECOND SOLDIER: Eh?

SPY: What I ordered.

SECOND SOLDIER: Oh, it's you . . . yes. . . . (*He produces a small packet or two surreptitiously.*)

SPY: Is this all?

SECOND SOLDIER: For the moment.

SPY: How much?

SECOND SOLDIER: Eight hundred.

SPY: Too much.

SECOND SOLDIER: They cost me almost that.

SPY (*takes them*): Put them on my account.

SECOND SOLDIER: But when——?

SPY: You will be paid. And—you have seen nothing. I never talked to you. I don't exist.

The SPY *vanishes into the Embassy, audience's right.*

FIRST SOLDIER: What's all that? Since when have you had commercial relations with the Russians?

SECOND SOLDIER: Even a fascist must live. I supply him with postcards.

FIRST SOLDIER: Who is he?

SECOND SOLDIER: Isn't it obvious?

GENERAL (*suddenly*): Men, I need your help.

FIRST SOLDIER: We're off duty.

GENERAL: We are all in the service of the god of love.

SECOND SOLDIER: But we can't live on our military pay alone.

GENERAL: Well, claim at the Ministry. Do as I do. (*Suddenly.*) What kind of mercenary prattle is this? Just now you shed a tear for them. Is it in the traditions of our country to confuse love with high finance?

SECOND SOLDIER: No, it isn't. That's what's wrong with us.

GENERAL: What did you say? Lef . . . wait for it, left turn. In step this time. This is war. Left-right-left.

They go, as though on parade, at the double. As another saint comes out to hit the clock, the face of the American Embassy is flown to reveal JULIET *sitting in an attitude of deep dejection in the small section of the drawing room shown. The door opens, and* MR AMBASSADOR MOULSWORTH *enters.*

MOULSWORTH: Well, and how's my girl? Tired, heh? Don't I get my kiss? Hey, I got news to put the sparkle back in your eye.

JULIET (*fiercely*): Dad, I've got to tell you.

MOULSWORTH (*good-humoured*): O.K., and I won't tell Freddie.

JULIET (*amazed*): You know, then?

MOULSWORTH: Sure, I saw you . . . and let me tell you, you looked just great . . . standing there in the moonlight in that Paris-type exclusive dress . . . and let me tell you something, the guy you were with . . . well, he was a tribute to your taste, and there's no reason on God's earth why Freddie should ever know . . .

JULIET (*pale*): You liked Igor?

MOULSWORTH: Who's that?

JULIET: The boy I was with.

MOULSWORTH: Yeah. Swell physique. Great golfer, I bet. What was his name again?

JULIET: Igor.

MOULSWORTH: Well, what's in a name? I had a classmate called Epiphany. Anyway, that's all over now. (*He beams.*) Now, listen to this baby. Are you ready?

JULIET (*emotional*): Pop, If you've got good news, give. Right now I need to hear it, but bad.

BEULAH MOULSWORTH *enters.*

BEULAH: Have you told her, Hooper?

MOULSWORTH (*tetchy*): I'm on the point of doing so, Beulah. Give a guy a break. (*Beaming.*) Great news, Julie——

BEULAH: And how's my daughter this morning? (*Smothers Juliet with kisses.*)

JULIET: Hi, Mom.

BEULAH: What have you said to her?

MOULSWORTH (*pointed*): Nothing, yet. (*Beaming.*) Great news, Julie——

BEULAH: Great news indeed. You're a big girl now——

MOULSWORTH (*with terrible patience*): Let me handle this, Beulah. Julie——

JULIET: Yes?

MOULSWORTH: Freddie.

JULIET: What about him?

MOULSWORTH: He's flying in on the midday clipper?

JULIET (*pale*): Oh, no . . . (*She faints.*)

BEULAH (*sarcastic*): You'll handle it, Beulah.

MOULSWORTH: What's the matter with her?

BEULAH: Get some water, Hooper. She's fainted.

MOULSWORTH: Fainted—that's impossible.

BEULAH: Get some water. There, there, mother's here, mother's here.

BEULAH *cradles Juliet in her arms.*

(*Loud.*) You're just the most tactful man I've ever met, that's all.

    MOULSWORTH *returns with a glass of water.*

MOULSWORTH: I am forthright. In Washington they call me Forthright Hoop Moulsworth. I've heard them.

BEULAH: Julie's a girl, Hooper. A girl. Girls don't go for forthrightness.

MOULSWORTH: How was I to know that?

BEULAH (*with an embarrassing sweetness*): Girls thrive on a lingering uncertainty . . . on a tremulous half-doubt . . . I know. I was a girl myself.

MOULSWORTH: Beulah . . . if I ran my business the way you think . . . How is she?

BEULAH: Coming round, oh so slowly. She's sensitive.

MOULSWORTH: We're all sensitive. (*Beaming.*) How's my honey?

JULIET (*softly*): Dad . . .

MOULSWORTH: Yeah, here I am, right here.

JULIET: I've got to tell you . . . I am not in love with Freddie.

MOULSWORTH: Not in——? Now, wait a minute.

BEULAH: She must have calm, Hooper.

MOULSWORTH: So must I have calm.

BEULAH: Up to bed, my only sweet one.

JULIET (*rising*): I'm going . . . but first I got to tell you . . . I'm in love with Igor.

BEULAH (*a girl again*): There's someone else. . . . What's he like?

JULIET: Dad saw him.

MOULSWORTH: Beulah, this is far too serious to accept as a matter of course. Remember, Freddie's flying out here at his own expense. Who is this other guy?

JULIET: Igor Vadimovitch Romanoff, the son of their Ambassador.

MOULSWORTH (*a great shout*): What?

JULIET (*quiet*): I'll go lie down now—get some rest, if I can.

    She goes out. Long pause.

BEULAH (*very quiet*): Maybe we didn't treat her right when she was a baby . . . maybe it's our fault——

MOULSWORTH (*rising, pale*): I guess there comes a time in the life of every parent——

BEULAH (*suddenly violent*): Oh, Hooper, this isn't a board meeting!

MOULSWORTH (*shouting back*): She must know what she's doing to me . . . her father? Why, if this ever gets out! It's impossible. I don't believe it ever happened. And you can sit there and tell me——

BEULAH: The fault, dear Brutus——

MOULSWORTH: Don't quote at me! (*Pause.*) Beulah. We summon all our resources of tact and understanding.

BEULAH: I was never sold on Freddie being right for her.

MOULSWORTH: That is neither here nor there. Freddie's father rowed in my boat at Princeton, but I'm deliberately forgetting all that—all my personal loyalties. The fact is that our only daughter has fallen for a Commie—a Communist, Beulah—and when I say Communist, Beulah, I don't mean a guy who sent a food package to the wrong side in Spain—I mean the son of a high-ranking Soviet executive!

BEULAH: You always show everything up in its worse possible light.

MOULSWORTH: Good God, Beulah, don't be such a damned fool.

BEULAH: Oh! that wicked temper of yours! First degree mental cruelty!

    Pause. MOULSWORTH *walks about.*

BEULAH: It may just be a girlish crush—a teenage urge.

MOULSWORTH: Julie's twenty.

BEULAH: Oh, Hooper, don't be so hideously unimaginative!

She never had any of the usual teenage urges. She may be starting late.

MOULSWORTH: Yeah, that's it, a juvenile infatuation. Of course. Why didn't we think of that before?

BEULAH: And then again—it may be love.

MOULSWORTH: I don't want that word mentioned again. Come, my dear, let us, you and I, go talk to her, calmly and with a modicum of dignity. What we cannot achieve by our persuasiveness, let us achieve by our example. After all, we are her parents, and the scriptures declare in no uncertain terms that we command her honour and her obedience. One thing only I wish you to promise me before we go up to our daughter.

BEULAH: And what is that?

MOULSWORTH: That you keep you mouth shut and let me do the talking.

They go. JULIET, *who appeared in the upstairs room soon after she left her parents, is lying on her bed in an attitude of tragic resignation. The façade of the Embassy falls as the façade of the other Embassy rises.* IGOR *stands. The* SPY *sits at a table, a few pieces of paper stretched before him.*

SPY: And?

IGOR: And . . . ? More I can't remember.

SPY: A confession of only eight pages? It appears as though you were still attempting to conceal something. (*Pause.*) Comrade Kotkov's recent confession ran to two hundred and fourteen type-written pages, and was written in a clear, concise, functional style. At the end, the reader had a vivid impression of the author's inner rottenness. It was a model of how such documents should be prepared. (*Pause.*) You have nothing to add? (*He sighs.*) Very well, let me help you. There are some comrades who can do nothing for themselves. Page eight, line twenty-three. You claim that love guided your deviation. (*He laughs.*) I had over-estimated your intelligence, Lieutenant.

IGOR: Because I speak the truth, no doubt.

SPY: Love recognizes frontiers, just as do armies.

IGOR: Only cynicism has no bounds.

SPY: Explain yourself.

IGOR: If my thoughts are simplified even further to suit your intellect, I shall soon be reciting the alphabet.

SPY (*deeply suspicious*): Which alphabet—ours or theirs?

IGOR (*exasperated*): Oh, my God!

SPY: What name did you mention?

IGOR: When?

SPY: God, did I hear?

IGOR: Why not?

SPY: Are you a believer?

IGOR: I have a perfect right to believe if I wish.

SPY: I did not ask you whether you had a right to believe. I asked you whether you do believe.

IGOR: I don't see the difference.

SPY: All the difference in the world. In the old days it was criminal to believe. With the advent of democracy, we are now given the choice of belief or disbelief, but naturally, we are put on our honour to make the right choice. Otherwise, democracy would have no meaning.

IGOR: Oh, the devil take you.

The SPY *immediately crosses himself.*

What are you doing?

SPY (*pleasantly, in spite of his nervousness*): Belief in the devil has never been forbidden by any regime.

The SOVIET AMBASSADOR *and* MRS ROMANOFF *enter.*

ROMANOFF: Good morning.

EVDOKIA: Good morning.

ROMANOFF: What is there for breakfast?

EVDOKIA: Caviar.

ROMANOFF: Caviar, caviar, caviar. Is there no end to this monotony? (*Hastily.*) I say this with all deference to our splendid sturgeon fisheries and our modern canneries.

SPY: One moment. Another subject has priority. Your Excellency, I must denounce your son.

ROMANOFF: Again?

EVDOKIA: Just a minute . Women have equality. I demand to speak first.

SPY: The fact that women have equality gives them no special privileges, as they have in the West. You cannot expect to enjoy both equality and the bourgeois myth of 'ladies first'.

EVDOKIA: I am the wife of an Ambassador. I have the right to speak first.

SPY: Only outside the Embassy. Within these walls the fact that I am your chauffeur is forgotten, and I revert to being a high ranking officer of the police.

ROMANOFF: Let him speak, Evdokia. It is more prudent. Let him denounce Igor before you denounce me.

EVDOKIA: How did you know I was going to denounce you?

ROMANOFF: No breakfast is complete without it.

SPY: Now——

IGOR: No! Let me denounce myself!

ROMANOFF (*warmly*): That's the spirit. That's my son.

IGOR: I am in love!

EVDOKIA (*scandalized*): A fine time you choose. I must say, with Junior Captain Marfa Vassilievna Zlotochienko arriving today.

IGOR: With who arriving?

EVDOKIA: Your betrothed. The heroic commander of the sloop *Dostoievsky*.

IGOR: My betrothed? But I've never even heard of her.

ROMANOFF: We intended to introduce her to you before the marriage.

IGOR: I should hope so.

ROMANOFF: Don't be ridiculous, and start behaving like a spoiled child. I met your mother for the first time at our wedding. There was no time for surprise. We were both spared the degradation of emotional behaviour.

IGOR: I refuse to marry this female!

EVDOKIA: You will do as you're told! We have noted with considerable regret that you are prone to unstable and introspective behaviour, and that at times you are as self-pitying as a fascist.

ROMANOFF: Evdokia, you are going too far!

EVDOKIA: Yes, and I know where he gets it from. Talking in your sleep about the imperial occasions in St Petersburg. St Petersburg, if you please, not even Petrograd.

SPY: Most interesting.

ROMANOFF (*a pathetic figure*): I don't believe you.

EVDOKIA: You even sang a snatch of the Imperial Anthem, and lay to attention in bed. Your abrupt movement made the eiderdown slide to the floor, and I had to get out of bed to pick it up.

ROMANOFF (*roused*): And what about you? Yesterday, when I took you shopping, you lingered a full quarter of an hour outside a shop displaying French hats.

SPY: Oh—ho!

EVDOKIA (*uncertain*): I did it to pour my scorn on them.

ROMANOFF: Yes, but while your mouth was muttering malice, your eye was roving avariciously over those odious shreds of tinsel. Deny it if you can—you were dying to try them on!

EVDOKIA (*after a terrible pause—a hunted woman*): Have I not suffered enough in my life without this? I was strong when I defied the Cossacks and carried vital messages under an arcade of knouts to the red sailors of the Baltic Fleet. I was strong when I distributed potato-soup to our troops through three days and nights without sleep. I have survived revolution, war, pestilence and famine. Have I now surrendered my dignity—to a hat?

SPY (*sly*): Well—have you?

EVDOKIA (*emotionally*): Yes, I have. I have! I admit it. I—I confess. It is a tiny confection made up of three black feathers, with a coronet of cheeky silver lace. (*Defiant.*) I love that hat! Last week they removed it from the window, and I was nearly ill. I retired to my bed and wept. I thought they had sold it. Yesterday, I passed the shop—and there it was again! My life suddenly held a new meaning for me. All unpleasantness was forgotten. I kissed my husband in the street.

ROMANOFF: Evdokia! That is how you gave yourself away. (*He kisses her on the forehead with emotion.*)

SPY: A most interesting revelation.

ROMANOFF: You underestimate us, my friend. Do you think that we are the only fallible beings here? What about this, which I discovered among your personal belongings? (*He produces an American Magazine from his pocket.*)

SPY (*trembling*): You have been through my suitcase?

ROMANOFF: You go through my desk every evening. I only returned the compliment. And what do I find? Decadent American magazines! Stories of drug addiction in Cincinnati! The adventures of lascivious space-men! And as if that were not sufficient—postcards of an indisputably suggestive nature, depicting the ruins of Pompeii in a most unscholarly light, and dwelling with shocking emphasis on the murky corridors of the Follies. Explain yourself, comrade.

SPY (*uncertain*): I collected this material in order to furnish the Party with proof of Western decadence.

ROMANOFF: The decadence of the West is well enough known by the Party not to need proof. Can you deny that these items constitute part of a vast and well-documented private collection?

SPY: I . . .

ROMANOFF (*ferociously*): Confess!

SPY (*with a cry*): Ah, that terrible word! (*Slowly—on his knees.*) I confess . . . but you cannot know the loneliness of a spy's life . . . everyone is frightened of me . . . women are only good and kind to me if they want me to overlook some indiscretion, and it's a calculated, a charmless, and a frightened love they give me. . . . (*He weeps.*) To me, women surrender everything but their secrets, and their company makes me feel more lonely than I feel alone.

ROMANOFF (*embarrassed*): Come, come, not before breakfast. Here's my handkerchief.

SPY: A handkerchief! When I could flood the Volga with my tears!

ROMANOFF (*with some pride*): There is no doubt about it. No nation can confess as magnificently or as completely as we.

SPY: Ah, the relief . . . the relief!

ROMANOFF: Now, now, you are a most distinguished secret agent. We will forget your little lapse.

SPY: No, no! Never forget it! Ah, my soul. How good it is to suffer so remorselessly.

ROMANOFF (*with some impatience*): What kind of architecture is this? One brick is displaced, and the entire edifice collapses.

IGOR: You have more experience than we have, father. You are older. I fall in love. The chauffeur gives in to his loneliness. Mother surrenders herself to a hat——

EVDOKIA (*burying her head in her hands*): My hat! What a disgrace. (*Suddenly horrified realization.*) And it isn't even my hat!

IGOR: You, father, you only let yourself go at night, when you dream of Leningrad.

ROMANOFF: Leningrad? St Petersburg. That is an historical fact, and not subversion. (*Dreamily.*) I remember the city in nineteen thirteen. The light streaming through the windows of the Winter Palace into the snow.

IGOR (*romantic*): You were outside, in the cold with the peasants.

ROMANOFF: I was inside, in the warmth, with the court—planning the revolution. I was the Party's inside man. My duties were to dance with the wives of army commanders, and surreptitiously find out the dispositions of their husband's units. It was delicious. . . .

IGOR: Then surely, father, with your experience, you can understand me when I tell you that I am in love—desperately, whole-heartedly, in love.

SPY: I understand you, brother.

EVDOKIA: Who is she? Some penniless local girl?

IGOR: Does it matter?

ROMANOFF: We—that is, your mother and I—wish you to marry well, my son, high up in the hierarchy.

IGOR: But that is snobbism!

EVDOKIA: Don't be ridiculous. Snobbism was abolished in nineteen seventeen.

IGOR: I am in love with the daughter of an Ambassador!

EVDOKIA (*ogling*): Just a moment. Which Ambassador?

IGOR: The Ambassador of the United States of America.

A terrible pause.

ROMANOFF (*his voice breaking with emotion*): Are you aware of the words you have just uttered?

IGOR (*standing stiffly to attention*): Yes, father. Otherwise I could not have uttered them.

ROMANOFF (*suddenly losing all control, screams*): Swine! (*Pause.*) Saboteur! (*Pause.*) Interventionist! (*Pause.*) Anarchist! (*Pause.*) Trotskyist! (*Pause—with a sob.*) My son!

During each of these accusations, it seems as though tears are being scattered round the room like grain. The AMBASSADOR, *scarlet with passion, shouts each word like a military order.*

SPY (*in ecstasy*): This surpasses all other confessions!

ROMANOFF (*contorted with fury and yet with traces of compassion and contrition, almost hopefully*): Can you change your mind?

IGOR (*stiff*): No, father.

ROMANOFF (*with ill-concealed pride in his son*): You will go up to your room.

IGOR: Yes, father.

ROMANOFF: Why do you smile?

IGOR: I will not be alone. (*He goes, stiffly.*)

ROMANOFF: You!

SPY: Me?

ROMANOFF: Breakfast is laid for three. You will join us.

EVDOKIA: A spy at the dining table?

ROMANOFF: Evdokia, we have lost our son.

EVDOKIA (*with a shriek*): Vadim!

ROMANOFF (*calm as ice*): Caviar, you said? Let us enjoy it. . . .

> As IGOR *appears upstairs, the façade falls. Two people enter the square, one a huge and cheerful* AMERICAN, *the other a pretty but grim* RUSSIAN GIRL. *They are followed by the* TWO SOLDIERS.

RUSSIAN GIRL: Thank you for allowing me to share your taxi.

AMERICAN (*gay*): That's O.K. Anything else I can do for you?

RUSSIAN GIRL (*cold*): No.

FIRST SOLDIER: Peanuts, traditional salted marzipan, raffia table-runners, English collar-studs, back numbers of *True Detective Magazine*?

SECOND SOLDIER: Keepsakes, bangles, prehistoric coins, religious postcards, beautifully picked out in silk and sequins?

RUSSIAN GIRL: You have no sociological novels?

FIRST SOLDIER: No.

AMERICAN: And no flowers?

SECOND SOLDIER: No.

AMERICAN (*gay*): Well, that's it. No flowers. (*Takes out a note.*) Give me something for that. Oh, anything. Bangles. Sure. That's fine. Just great. Do I get any change? O.K., I know the answer to that one. Americans. No change.

RUSSIAN GIRL (*studying him keenly*): You are not thrifty.

AMERICAN: I'm in love.

RUSSIAN GIRL: All the more reason for thrift.

AMERICAN: See you, beautiful.

RUSSIAN GIRL: Goodbye, sir.

> *They go to their respective Embassies, and enter. The* GENERAL *tiptoes quickly on to the stage.*

GENERAL: Who were they?

FIRST SOLDIER: Search me.

SECOND SOLDIER: The plot thickens.

Vaguely, like a chant, the words 'Romanoff' and 'Juliet' can be heard, very softly.

JULIET: Romanoff.

IGOR: Juliet.

GENERAL: Sh! What's that?

FIRST SOLDIER: I can't hear——

GENERAL: Listen.

JULIET: Romanoff.

IGOR: Juliet.

FIRST SOLDIER: Ho—yes.

JULIET: Romanoff.

IGOR: Juliet.

SECOND SOLDIER: It sounds like . . . Romanoff . . .

FIRST SOLDIER: And . . . Juliet?

GENERAL (*very softly*): Where's it coming from?

FIRST SOLDIER (*near one Embassy*): Up here.

GENERAL: Balconies . . . ? Then there's hope . . .

The figure of Death the Reaper wobbles out and strikes the bell.

FIRST SOLDIER: It's Death!

GENERAL: Death again? Death at a quarter to nine?

FIRST SOLDIER: . . . Eight thirty-three?

SECOND SOLDIER: . . . Nine fourteen?

GENERAL: It's the first time I've ever known Death make a mistake.

CURTAIN

ACT TWO

Noon to afternoon.

It is later in the day. The light is no longer the pale silver of early morning, but has the deep orange glow which makes the sky intensely blue and the walls the colour of peaches. As the curtain rises the clock strikes three. The Embassy walls rise slowly. Both lower rooms are empty, but the upper rooms are occupied by JULIET *and* IGOR. *They are both in positions of romantic dejection. The* TWO SOLDIERS *lie lazily in the street. It is siesta time. One is asleep, the other strums lazily on a guitar. Their merchandize lies by their side.*

JULIET *is the first to come slowly to life.*

JULIET: Oh, why must the mind hover, a blind bee, over dead flowers? And yet, maybe I like my flowers dead . . . maybe I'm not the happy, open-minded daughter parents dream about . . . maybe I'm not the normal, healthy modern girl who makes a sane selection of a mate after mature consideration in a night club . . . Do I betray my age group by thinking? Am I old fashioned . . . and just meant for tragedy? (*With profound self-pity, and a sudden interest.*) . . . Oh, perhaps tragedy. (*She looks at photo of Freddie.*) To look at a man . . . to visualize children with his eyes and my nose . . . Oh, Freddie, if only I hated you . . . but no, I like you . . . quite . . . in your silly, keen, determined way . . . I never quite know what you're being determined about, but that look makes older men call you promising. Freddie, you're a skyscraper of a guy. You'll hold your babies in all the right positions . . . You'll teach them baseball before they can walk and you'll teach them to count before they can read . . . only Freddie . . . I won't be those babies' mother . . . why? Because I like you, dear . . . and because I don't love you . . . (*She drops the photo, and takes up an empty frame.*) Igor, I love you . . . but I don't really like you much . . . maybe the two don't go together . . . when I was small, I always swore I'd marry a man with blue eyes . . . your eyes are brown . . . brown like damp patches on the wall, like school-book covers . . . and yet, when I look into them, I lose my way . . . I forget my discretion, my education, my table-manners . . . (*She holds the empty frame close to her face and shuts her eyes.*) Oh Igor, the way the warmth creeps into those eyes against your better judgement . . . like a slow wave of sunshine washing up a pasture late on a winter afternoon . . . made more welcome by surprise . . .

    She is lost in her reverie, and cries quietly. IGOR *stirs and leaps to his feet with the violence of a romantic.*

IGOR: Theory is a corset. I can no longer breathe. Was Karl Marx ever in love? Are there frontiers which even the greatest of teachers have never crossed? Would the barricades have attracted so many martyrs if love had been as easy to find as death? I wonder. . . . For the first time in my life, I feel a coward. I love the sea, but I love a woman more. A woman? If I could take her home—if it were possible— they would criticize her frivolous and untheoretical mind. How I hate myself at times. They would even criticize her looks—that vapidly romantic expression—those great grey eyes which ask endless questions, and which make me smile as I think of them—that concern with dress, with personal appearance—so unfeminine . . . and yet . . . as one who has been nurtured on the truth, the accurate, didactic truth, I must shout for the good of my Slavonic soul, 'I am in love!' If I have to die for it, if I have to kiss the soil with frozen lips, I shall have known this exultation . . . and Juliet, the silences . . . ! Stretching so intimately into infinity, silences which seem to wander among the stars and among stray thoughts, reducing all mysteries to the shape of a sweet and knowing smile, exalting each tremulous flicker of an eyelash to a vast, unfathomable mystery. Juliet . . . the tender gravity of our silences! (*He turns his head away violently.*) Oh, how undignified to feel the hot tears rolling down where rain and sleet hammer so ineffectually! Remember, in your lucid moments, Igor Vadimovitch Romanoff, that you are second-in-command of a warship. . . .

He stands stiffly to attention—his back to the audience—then breaks his stance, and says brokenly.

No, Igor Vadimovitch Romanoff . . . there are no lucid moments left . . . you are a man in love. . . . (*He sits heavily.*)

JULIET (*with sudden anger*): Oh, drink your vodka with your buddies. What do you care if I'm on the verge of suicide? You probably chalk up the number of your conquests on the hull of your ice-breaker. I can see you now, joking with your awful poppa about how you insinuated your way into a reactionary's heart. I hate you! (*She picks up Freddie's photograph.*) Poor Freddie . . . I said such heartless things about you. . . . (*She studies the photograph with compassion and tenderness.*) Oh, Freddie, you're dreadful. . . . (*She drops the photograph again.*) Forgive me . . . Igor, Freddie . . . both of you . . . I'm not . . . myself. . . . (*She relapses again.*)

IGOR (*he rises angrily*): And yet I doubt whether you have the capacity to suffer as I can suffer . . . you come from a new and superficial race . . . we have suffered from time immemorial, and when necessary, we fall into the bitter practice gracefully and unnoticeably . . . no doubt you are seeking consolation with your father, who is successfully cheering you up by recounting his exploits on the Stock Exchange . . . it is your education I must blame, not you . . . I know my duty . . . I will suffer for us both. . . . (*He sits and suffers.*)

JULIET (*a murmur*): Oh Igor . . . Igor . . . Igor.

IGOR (*a murmur*): Juliet . . . Juliet . . . Juliet.

They are lost in darkness as HOOPER, BEULAH *and* FREDDIE *enter the downstairs room.*

FREDDIE: Well, when's the next plane back?

MOULSWORTH: You seem to take the whole ghastly situation very lightly, if you don't mind my saying so.

FREDDIE: I take it easy, sir. I've never forced anyone to do anything they didn't want to do. Hell, a girl can change her mind about a guy. I've changed my mind about a good number of girls.

BEULAH: Oh, it's all too dreadful . . . and to think that Freddie has flown . . . How many miles is it, Freddie?

FREDDIE: Four thousand.

BEULAH: Four thousand miles!

MOULSWORTH: That figure is beginning to annoy me, Beulah. We've had it several times already. You've even consulted an atlas.

FREDDIE: I made it four thousand two hundred and seventeen miles, counting the trips to the airport. But what the hell. I I like flying.

MOULSWORTH: Exactly. He likes flying, Beulah. Now, I knew your father, son.

FREDDIE: I know you did, sir . . . and he knew you.

MOULSWORTH: He did indeed . . . and what's more . . . I liked him.

FREDDIE: I never talked about it with him, sir . . . But I'm pretty certain he liked you.

MOULSWORTH (*a little irritated*): I talked to him about it. He did like me. He liked me a lot. He was a fine, upstanding man, and the best Number Three ever to row for Princeton. Now, young man, let me tell you right here from the shoulder what your father would have done under those circumstances. He'd have gone up those stairs and he'd have shouted his way into the girl's heart.

FREDDIE: I beg to differ with you, sir. Dad was a gentleman. He'd never have raised his voice against a lady.

BEULAH (*in triumph*): There!

MOULSWORTH (*to his wife*): What are you so happy about? Just stabbing me in the back all the way down the line.

FREDDIE: Dad would have gone right out there and clobbered that Russian.

BEULAH: Ho, how romantic!

FREDDIE: Yes, ma'am, he was of the 'let-the-best-man-win' school. He always won. He weighed 'most three hundred pounds.

BEULAH: Maybe that's the solution. Women just adore brave men. Look at the bullfighters.

MOULSWORTH: What the hell have bullfighters got to do with it? D'you think I want an international incident on my hands?

FREDDIE: No, and then I'm not a scrapper. I studied law for half a year. I'm a firm believer in negotiation.

MOULSWORTH: Good God, man. The days of negotiation for a wife are over. Nowadays marriage like everything else is strictly business, and business is pressure. Go up there, son, and fight for your wife. Start shouting, or you'll lose her to the next customer.

FREDDIE: Mrs Moulsworth.

BEULAH: Yes, dear?

FREDDIE: I'll do anything you think wise within reason. I'm deeply attached to your daughter, but I think it only fair to tell you that when I asked her to marry me she never said more in reply than that she'd think it over.

MOULSWORTH: In business that's tantamount to an acceptance. She may argue the terms of the contract, but she's initialled the rough draft, that's how I see it. Son, go up there and clinch that deal.

BEULAH: Oh, Hooper, do stop seeing everything in terms of business. When he proposed to me, he slapped me on the back, and said, 'Beulah, how about going into partnership?' Then when Juliet came, I woke up to find him standing at the foot of the bed with some flowers. The first words I heard him utter as I came out of the haze and the agony were 'Well, first one off the production line.'

MOULSWORTH: Well, I got you, didn't I? That just proves my point.

BEULAH (*her eyes shut in exquisite suffering*): There is such a thing in life as beauty, Hooper. It's a very wonderful thing. And your life has been the poorer for the lack of it.

MOULSWORTH (*loud*): I like beauty when it's practical, Beulah. I like a beautiful swimming pool, but only if it's got water in it. I like a beautiful marriage, but I'll still breathe a whale of a sigh of relief when both parties have said 'I do'. Now, son, are you going to let me down?

FREDDIE (*good-naturedly*): I hate to say this to you, sir, but it's my marriage, not yours.

MOULSWORTH: No, sir. The blue chips are down. I'm talking to you and appealing to you as one good American to another. Julie's a girl we both love and cherish, I as a father, you as a man who found it in himself to propose marriage to her. Son, she's drifting out of our life. She's in love with a Communist. If this thing goes through, it may mean that she could be guilty of attempting to destroy the government of the United States by force.

FREDDIE: Oh, that's ridiculous.

MOULSWORTH: It may sound ridiculous to you and to me, but it won't sound so ridiculous before a Federal Investigating Committee; and that's what we'd have to face, all of us . . . indictments, suspicions . . . ruin . . . and all because of her stubbornness. . . .

FREDDIE: Well, what d'you want me to do, sir? Talk to her? Or marry her?

MOULSWORTH (*after a short pause*): Whatever you think best, son. You're right. I was kind of hasty and . . . well, I'm a little sore about what has happened. . . . It all seemed so great before breakfast. . . .

FREDDIE (*with a grave, deep sigh*): I guess that's . . . life.

MOULSWORTH (*with a reciprocal sigh*): Never said a truer word, son. That's what it is. Life. The mighty Unpredictable.

FREDDIE: Just at the start of the home run, why, you have to break your ankle.

MOULSWORTH: Precisely right.

FREDDIE (*rising*): Well, I'll go up there. Talk to her.

MOULSWORTH (*extending his hand, moved*): That's my boy. Put it there.

BEULAH (*who has been lost in a profound reverie*): One small question, Freddie. If she changes her mind and wants to have you, what will you do?

FREDDIE: Oh, I'll marry her. I believe in marriage, Mrs Moulsworth.

BEULAH: And do you believe in love?

FREDDIE (*as though it were unimportant*): Sure, sure.

BEULAH: Then go up there, and our blessings go with you. Freddie, be gentle.

MOULSWORTH: Yeah, be gentle, but don't forget to be real tough.

    FREDDIE *goes*.

MOULSWORTH: Goddam gutless generation. If it wasn't for the fact that I'm a diplomat, I'd have shot my mouth off. His girl going to marry a Red, and he talks about negotiation where possible, all six foot six of him sits there looking solemn and pious, talking of negotiation where possible.

BEULAH: He's very sensitive.

MOULSWORTH: You always say that. A little mousy guy I can understand being sensitive, but a guy his size just hasn't the right.

BEULAH: Sh!

    They both look at the ceiling. FREDDIE *has knocked at Juliet's door.* JULIET *stirs.*

FREDDIE: Julie . . . it's me . . . Freddie.

JULIET: Go away, Freddie, . . . I'm not in a state to see anybody.

FREDDIE: I only wanted to say goodbye, kid ... I've come four thousand miles to say it.

JULIET: D'you mean that?

FREDDIE: Sure. I understand.

JULIET: Are you alone?

FREDDIE: I swear it.

JULIET: I'll let you in for a moment, Freddie, if you promise not to look at me.

FREDDIE: That's a tough assignment but ... I promise.

She unlocks the door. FREDDIE *enters.*

Julie!

JULIET (*her back to him*): You promised!

FREDDIE: Sure. Well I—well, there's really not much to say.

JULIET: How's business?

FREDDIE: How the hell do I know? Dad bought up 'most all his competitors before he died. There's nothing left for me to do.

JULIET: You mean you've gone sour on refrigerators?

FREDDIE: I guess I'm just ... mature. (*Sees his photograph.*) Hey, where d'you get that awful photograph?

JULIET: I don't know ... I had it.

FREDDIE: No wonder you fell out of love.

JULIET (*pained and weary*): Is Dad very upset?

FREDDIE: Yes ... I guess he is ... (*Without much enthusiasm.*) He's a great guy.

JULIET (*dull*): The greatest. What can I do?

FREDDIE (*he smiles*): I know what I'd do, but then I'm not you, and I don't think any advice of mine would be much value to you.

JULIET (*to him for the first time, with a kind of interest*): Freddie, you've changed.

FREDDIE (*with charm*): Have I? (*Not looking at her.*) Hey, Julie, what's it like being in love? Really in love?

JULIET: Hell.

FREDDIE: Is that so? Gee, I'm sorry.

JULIET: What are you going to do now?

FREDDIE: Oh, I don't know. Marry. Settle down.

JULIET: Anyone in mind?

FREDDIE (*smiling*): Never less than six. Put it down to my business training.

JULIET: I envy all six.

FREDDIE: That's sweet of you.

> Pause. *But during this pause:*

BEULAH: They're talking. I can hear the voices.

MOULSWORTH: That's not talk, that's mumbling. He'll never get to first base that way.

FREDDIE: D'you want me to go?

JULIET: Not particularly.

FREDDIE: I think maybe I ought to anyway.

JULIET: Aren't you going to tell me I'm crazy and unpatriotic to fall for a Commie?

FREDDIE: No, I'm not going to tell you that. You're the only person can convince yourself of that.

JULIET: God knows I've tried, Freddie.

FREDDIE: Yeah, I think you have.

JULIET: These barriers ought not to exist.

FREDDIE: Sure, there ought to be no more wars, no religious intolerance, no race discrimination, no bombs—everyone in his right mind thinks that, and yet somehow, when we all get together, we find all these things are still there, and just a bit worse than before.

JULIET (*with a trace of humour*): You're not very helpful.

FREDDIE: I know it.

JULIET: I don't know what's happened to you, Freddie. You've started to think.

FREDDIE: Sure. It was tough, but I made it.

JULIET: And you're a bit of a pessimist.

FREDDIE (*with a vast smile*): Me, a pessimist? Not while there's baseball. Don't matter where I am, Paris, France, or this place, I have the scores phoned through to me every day.

JULIET (*affectionately*): There's my boy.

FREDDIE: Yeah. One thing about baseball. It never lets you down.

JULIET: I'm sorry, dear.

FREDDIE (*lightly*): That's O.K.

JULIET (*after a pause*): D'you want to kiss me?

FREDDIE: No. I know when I'm licked.

JULIET (*very upset*): Freddie!

FREDDIE: It wouldn't have worked, kid. You feel too strongly for me, know what I mean? I could never get as upset as you do, and that'd only upset me. I don't talk good, but you know what I mean. There'd be days with my great corny smile and the way I talk, well, it'd only irritate you. I really need a girl who doesn't want much out of life but what she sees . . . a girl who likes luxury but doesn't show it all the time. . . you see, I've got my problems too. Money's a hell of a thing to inherit. (*He rises.*) See you, Julie. Oh, I bought you some bangles off a guy in the street. I don't suppose you want them though.

JULIET: No, I don't . . . yes, give me them . . . they'll remind me of the dearest, sweetest guy I ever went with.

FREDDIE: I came out here with a brand new custom-made morning suit for my wedding . . . I'll go home alone, but remembered by a bangle . . . well, like I always say, that's life . . . I'll see you some place sometime . . . maybe you'll bring your husband over to see us . . . the kids can play in the pool. . . .

JULIET (*crying*): Don't, Freddie. . . .

FREDDIE: God bless you, baby. Keep pitching.

He leaves her. She just stands, immobile.

BEULAH: That was the door, Hooper. Listen! They're both coming down the stairs. I can hear four feet.

MOULSWORTH: You'd better be right.

BEULAH (*gentle*): Well, take that pioneering look off your face.

MOULSWORTH *smiles with some difficulty. His smile vanishes much more easily as* FREDDIE *re-enters alone.*

MOULSWORTH: Well?

FREDDIE: Well, I talked to her . . . (*He lights a cigarette.*)

MOULSWORTH: We are waiting to hear what you said.

BEULAH: Freddie, what did *she* say?

FREDDIE: I don't know that we have a right to judge her.

MOULSWORTH (*incredulous*): What was that?

FREDDIE: You see, sir . . . Mrs Moulsworth . . . I don't think
I've ever seen anyone in love before . . .

BEULAH: Then it's . . . real?

FREDDIE: Oh sure. Talking to her is about as hard as talking in
church. Everything you say, why, you get a feeling you're
interrupting even when you're not. When I knew her, she
was pretty. Now, she's beautiful. I can't explain it better'n
that.

BEULAH (*her handkerchief to her cheek*): I know what you want to
say, Freddie. I am a woman . . . and a mother. (*Suddenly
surprised by the silence of her husband.*) Hooper?

MOULSWORTH (*who has sat down heavily*): All the values of
human conduct which I have learned to respect lie scattered
around me. I just don't recognize anybody or anything any
more. I'm just not fit to continue, that's all. I'm an old timer,
a has-been.

FREDDIE: Once again, sir . . . I guess that's life.

MOULSWORTH (*snarling*): It's nothing of the sort, it's a goddam disaster. Young man, there's no plane back to Miami
until tomorrow morning. You're welcome to stay here,
only keep out of my sight.

BEULAH (*conciliatory*): Hooper . . .

MOULSWORTH (*violent*): You too.

The façade falls as the other rises. The other FAMILY is in
session. MARFA ZLOTOCHIENKO is holding forth, and appears to be
in full control.

MARFA (*blonde and ferocious*): I shall be forced to report un-
favourably on the state of this Embassy when I return. Your
Secret Service man is in tears. No man who is in the habit of

clouding his vision with tears can be consistently vigilant.

SPY (*elated*): On the contrary, I am only just beginning to see! How can one understand our great and tortured history except through the magnifying glass of tears?

MARFA: Disgraceful. You, Comrade Ambassador, are guilty of indisputable apathy, and you, Comrade, who should be a mirror in which your husband can see his errors are but the distorted glass of the fun fair. As for your son—marriage is, of course, out of the question. It is totally unrealistic to embark on marriage with widowhood as imminent.

ROMANOFF (*rising*): You can't mean what you are saying!

MARFA: What is the fate of the sleeping sentry? You are all asleep at your posts!

ROMANOFF: Evdokia! What has happened to you since we left Moscow?

EVDOKIA: We are traitors.

ROMANOFF: But why? Why? My son, you, me—is the rottenness in ourselves?

SPY (*with staring, happy eyes*): I shall become a monk, that's what I will do—and place my tremendous capacity for patience at the disposal of meditation and the illumination of manuscripts.

ROMANOFF: There you are, it is contagious. Why?

EVDOKIA: If this means Siberia or death—I shall go out and buy that hat today—I have already telephoned the shop and asked them to reserve it for me—I must have a few hours of pleasure.

ROMANOFF: It must be this confounded country which is subversive—the climate—the atmosphere—(*To* MARFA.) Why do you look so sarcastic? You can know nothing about this country, you have only just arrived here.

MARFA: On the contrary, I am extremely well informed about it. Conditions are chaotic, owing to a moribund economy, the atmosphere is one of sleepy indolence, and the climate is torrid in winter and more torrid in summer.

ROMANOFF: But . . . you have not lived through these summer nights.

MARFA: Summer nights? Of course I have, in the Black Sea. My eye never left the compass.

ROMANOFF (*exasperated*): All your life you have seen nothing except that which met your eye, and you have noticed nothing except that which has been brought to your attention.

MARFA: Your insults do not affect me, Comrade. I am sure that I know more about this country than you do, in spite of your ambassadorial pretensions. What is the annual rainfall of the capital?

ROMANOFF: I haven't any idea, nor do I think that it affects the political situation.

MARFA: Three millimetres.

ROMANOFF: Thank you very much. I'm sure that the information will prove most valuable.

MARFA: And how many kilometres of narrow-gauge railroads are there?

ROMANOFF: I don't know. We walk.

MARFA: Six point seven, with another five which has been under construction since nineteen twelve. And how many many secondary schools are there?

ROMANOFF: One.

MARFA: None.

ROMANOFF: Near enough.

MARFA: On the contrary. A hundred per cent error. So don't tell me that I notice nothing but that which has been brought to my attention. I inform myself about everything, and as a consequence I am able to speak with authority. As for you, your Excellency, you are precisely the type of old-style foreign representative which Honoured Artist K. K. Bolshikov attacked so brilliantly in his five-act drama *Kill the Swine*.

ROMANOFF: A subtle title.

MARFA: You speak of subtlety as though it were a virtue.

ROMANOFF: It is a mark of intelligence. (*He studies her.*) Strange to have such a beautiful face, disfigured from inside.

MARFA: Are you criticizing me?

ROMANOFF: We have a perfect right to criticize each other. It is a pastime encouraged by the Party. You have been criticizing me since your arrival. Now it's my turn. My criticism will take the form of a history lesson. Don't interrupt me—I am sure you know many more dates than I do, but I know more about our revolution than you do, because I was there! I remember the first glimmer of hope on a horizon which had been dead for years, no larger than a feather floating on the sea, but it was enough. I am not a religious man, but I used to go to church to hear the voices. There is no people which can sing as we can, and when the liberated passion of a thousand hearts streams into the golden dome, clashing, weaving, murmuring, roaring, then a man can believe in anything, for our battle cry is ecstasy. Some nations surpass themselves out of love, others out of hatred, others by contemplating the still waters of reason. We immortalize ourselves by ecstasy—and when the people saw that flicker of hope, they sang, millions of them, and made the sky more resonant than the cathedral roof. I saw expressions in the crowd which I shall never forget, the upturned eyes of dirty Byzantine angels, the smiles of women who believe in a truth so simple it defies description. The machine guns chattered in the cold, laughing victims fell painlessly to their death, the snow was stained with blood. Other voices took up the song, other feet stepped forward, other hands grasped home-made weapons. In the morning victory was ours, and many of the dead were smiling still. Those were the days of our enthusiasm. And what has happened since? Our land has become a huge laboratory, a place of human test-tubes. Our language, so rich, so masculine, so muscular, is but a pale shadow of its possibilities. Our literature, which ravished the dark soul of man with such pity, is now mobilized to serve an empty optimism. Our music, divorced from sadness, and the twilight, has lost its anchor in an ocean of dreariness. You, my dear child, were born into this monotonous nursery, and you have never played with other toys than boredom, pride and smugness. I blame you for nothing. You know nothing. You are nothing. And worse, you are no one. Do with us what you will. I have rediscovered my enthusiasm, and I will know how to laugh, even in death.

EVDOKIA (*emotional*): Vadim! We have a fine son!

Before the pale Marfa can say anything, EVDOKIA *and* VADIM *embrace with passion.* MARFA *goes out.*

SPY (*with eyes sparkling*): Love must spread like a plague. . . . Oh God, save those who have been immunized against emotion . . . help those who marvel at figures of wheat production, but who do not pause to marvel at an ear of corn.

MARFA *reappears above.*

MARFA: Lieutenant Romanoff!

IGOR (*waking from his gloom*): Who are you?

MARFA: Junior Commander Marfa Vassilievana Zlotochienko.

IGOR (*with a wan smile*): Oh, my wife. Are you blonde or brunette, thin or immensely fat?

MARFA: It is my duty to inform you that owing to the scandalous and anti-democratic attitude of your entire family, I will be forced to return by the first aeroplane to-morrow morning, and will further be forced to denounce the staff of this Embassy for anarchistic and fascist tendencies in surrendering to emotionalism of the most dangerous and subversive variety.

IGOR *starts laughing happily, almost hysterically.* MARFA *is taken aback, as though slapped in the face. The* PARENTS *break from their embrace, the* SPY *from his prayer.*

EVDOKIA (*gaily*): It's him laughing . . . Igor . . .

ROMANOFF (*delighted*): Yes . . .

They laugh. The GENERAL *has reappeared in the street, and listens, surprised, as the front of the Embassy descends. The* SOLDIERS *stir. The light begins to lose its lustre. The* GENERAL *is dressed formally with top hat, gloves, a walking stick and a portfolio.*

GENERAL: What a curious noise!

SECOND SOLDIER (*yawning*): It's the Russians laughing.

GENERAL (*surprised*): Yes. Have you noticed anything? Has anyone entered or come out of the Embassies?

FIRST SOLDIER: No. There's a seasonal slackness of business which lasts all the year round.

SECOND SOLDIER: You're pretty warmly dressed for this weather, General.

GENERAL (*weary*): It's not without reason that diplomats wear this kind of costume. Gloves, walking stick, portfolio, three articles to leave behind, if necessary.

FIRST SOLDIER: Are you going in there?

GENERAL: I have been summoned to both Embassies at the same hour, and accepted both engagements in a fit of absentmindedness. What is the time?

SECOND SOLDIER: What's the use of asking us? There hasn't been a saint in sight for the past couple of hours. (*He looks at the clock.*) They must be having an argument in there.

FIRST SOLDIER: Listen!

There is a hiss of machinery. THREE SAINTS *appear very quickly, strike each other in the confusion, and disappear at high speed.*

That's called making up for lost time.

GENERAL: I came here with plenty of time in hand. Now I suddenly find myself in a desperate hurry. Men, I've had an idea. You remember this morning when Death made a mistake?

FIRST SOLDIER   ⎱ Yes.
SECOND SOLDIER ⎰

GENERAL: Why shouldn't Death really make a mistake? Couldn't it be that our old friend up there was just dropping us a gentle hint? And isn't it possible that our Fatherland not only corrupts the living by making them oblivious of time, place, even of hatred—but that it makes even Death lazy and forgetful of his solemn duties? You don't follow. Human nature being what it is, legend and literature are full to over-flowing with tragic lovers—there's hardly a couple who don't end up horizontal, bloody and fruitless. Why should that be? What is the point of suffering if you can't survive afterwards to enjoy the relief?

SECOND SOLDIER: I told you, if we weren't so weak, we could threaten the two Governments responsible for their unhappiness.

GENERAL: Don't make light of our weaknesses. These days you have to be very strong to allow yourself the luxury of being weak.

FIRST SOLDIER: What do you suggest?

GENERAL: A trick! The prerogative of the weak. Tonight we celebrate the Royal Marriage of our Boy King Theodore the Uncanny to the Infanta of Old Castile in thirteen eleven, which led to the coalition of Saragossa, and the eventual expulsion of the Albanians from our soil.

SECOND SOLDIER: Steady sir, that's not till next Friday— and you said this morning that it was the Lithuanians who were driven out a thousand years ago tonight.

GENERAL: Did I?

SECOND SOLDIER: Yes.

GENERAL: Well, the great virtue of history is that it is adaptable. I have a very definite reason for wishing tonight to be the celebration of a wedding, with the symbolic blessing of two papier-mâché dummies by the Archbishop. So shall we say that with the help of the Spaniards we drove the Lithuanians out?

FIRST SOLDIER: Doesn't sound very probable.

GENERAL: The pretext hardly matters. It's the celebration which people enjoy. Unfortunately even Easter has become

largely a matter of eggs. Now kindly serenade the young
lady with an apt folk-song . . . a melancholy one. Don't
overdo it . . . not tragic . . . just melancholy.

FIRST SOLDIER
SECOND SOLDIER } (*sing softly with guitar accompaniment.*)

> Oh, won't someone open the door of the cage
> And set the bluebird free?
> Set it free. Set it free.
> It was caught in the spring, at a tender age
> It languished in summer, forgot how to sing
> In the autumn it lost the use of one wing
> Before winter comes and wild winds sting
> Set it free. Set it free.
> Set the bluebird free.

JULIET *appears sadly and inquisitively on her balcony.*

JULIET (*drab, with a little smile*): Oh, it's you.

GENERAL: Miss Moulsworth. Greetings. Listen to me. It is
extremely urgent. I need your help.

JULIET: You need *my* help?

GENERAL: Yes. If you wish to see the Lieutenant again, you
must do as I tell you.

JULIET: What do you want me to do?

GENERAL: Sh! Not so loud. I want you to knot the sheets of
your bed, and to hang them from your balcony.

JULIET (*with some enthusiasm*): Like I did when I ran away from
school?

GENERAL (*with excessive delight*): Did you? Yes. (*Conspiratorial
again*). Then I want you to write a farewell letter to your
parents.

JULIET: What? Oh, I couldn't. As though I was going to—no.
Dad's got a weak heart.

GENERAL: You surprise me. Couch the letter in somewhat
ambiguous terms. There's no need to mention the possi-
bility of any rash act—just thank them for all they've done

for you and say that you have run away to join the man you love.

JULIET: Even that might kill Dad.

GENERAL: The fact that you're happy?

JULIET: The fact that I didn't consult him first.

GENERAL: Really, I am running a little short of sympathy for him, Miss Moulsworth.

JULIET: He's a darling really . . . at heart.

GENERAL: Must I doubt that you are really in love?

JULIET (*hotly*): You've no right to doubt that, after what I've been through.

GENERAL: Then do as I tell you, and you will spread happiness round you like a cloak. You must trust me.

FIRST SOLDIER: You must trust him!

SECOND SOLDIER: Be a sport!

JULIET (*doubtful*): Well . . .

GENERAL: It is a matter of life and death . . . for several people . . . don't let your parents go into old age with you on their conscience. It isn't fair. It isn't Christian.

JULIET: Yes, that's a thought. O.K, I'll do it.

GENERAL: You won't regret it.

JULIET *goes in.*

FIRST SOLDIER: What now?

GENERAL: Another folk-song . . . something maritime . . . something about a sailor.

FIRST SOLDIER ⎱
SECOND SOLDIER ⎰

    Sailor where are you? are you?
    Is the storm on the sea, is the storm in your heart?
    Which of these storms keeps us apart?
    Sailor where are you? are you?
    Are you faithless or dead.
    Are the clouds in the sky, are the clouds in your head?
    Sailor, my sailor, we'll never be wed.
    Sailor where are you . . .

IGOR *appears on his balcony, a haggard figure, holding a revolver.*

IGOR: Why do you interrupt me?

GENERAL: Great heavens, Lieutenant Romanoff, what is that in your hand?

IGOR: A revolver. The classic solution to misery.

GENERAL: Are you aware that they are forbidden by law?

IGOR: How do you commit suicide then?

GENERAL: There are many other, less dangerous, methods.

IGOR (*lifting it*): You are too late.

GENERAL: Lieutenant, you will see Juliet tonight.

IGOR (*with a bitter laugh*): Really? Do you believe in the hereafter?

GENERAL: I believe in the herein.

IGOR: What's that?

GENERAL: Life as it is lived, with all its little annoyances.

IGOR: Little annoyances? You have never suffered.

GENERAL: No, and I don't intend to. Lieutenant, do something for me before you die.

IGOR: What?

GENERAL: Write a farewell letter to your parents.

IGOR: I have already done so. It covers seventeen pages. Then I ran out of ink.

GENERAL: And, Lieutenant, will you tie the sheets of your bed together, and then fix them to the balcony?

IGOR: As though I were running away?

GENERAL: Yes—No! As though you were advancing to happiness.

IGOR: I am an officer, sir. I am incapable of cowardice.

GENERAL: I understand your prejudice, sir, since, believe it or not, I am an officer myself. I am incapable of almost everything, but at the moment I do happen to know what I am talking about. If you wish to see Juliet again, alive, well, happy, do as I tell you. Give me a startling demonstration of seaman's knots.

IGOR: I cannot. My mind is made up.

The SPY *sidles out of the Embassy, then rushes up to the General.*

GENERAL (*horrified*):What do you want?

SPY (*desperate*): I am on your side. Help me, and I will help you.

GENERAL: What do you want?

SPY: Asylum.

GENERAL: Granted.

SPY: And——

GENERAL : What?

SPY: A letter of introduction to the most austere, the most rigid and terrible monastery in your country.

GENERAL: We will send you to the Mauve Friars. They never sit or stand. They walk about on their knees.

SPY (*Grasping the General's hand and kissing it rapturously*): Oh, equisite. My eternal gratitude.

IGOR *is about to shoot. The* GENERAL *sees this.*

GENERAL: Quick!

SPY: 'Last night we were as one, creatures in a dream, selflessly united in an endless waltz. From now on we are opposed, a man and a woman in love, the greatest, most exhausting struggle in the world, two moths racing for the flame, two cannibals devouring each other.'

IGOR (*limp, he lets the revolver drop with a clatter*): Farewell, reso-lution. How did you remember that?

SPY: I listened in the shadows, and took it down in shorthand. Then as I read it in my room at night, I began to feel lonely again, and jealous that such phrases should not have been addressed to me.

IGOR: Jealous? Am I capable of inspiring jealousy? Even in my present condition?

SPY: Oh yes, brother . . . yes . . . your life is still before you, even if it only lasts ten minutes . . . while I must expiate my sins in endless penance and terrifying disciplines.

IGOR (*with a little sigh of relief*): What a fool I am . . . we must rely on one another to understand ourselves. What did you want? Ah yes. Sheets. Is it for some joke?

GENERAL: Yes, yes, a joke.

IGOR: I like jokes. (*He goes.*)

SPY: Now—your part of the bargain.

GENERAL: Boys, take this gentleman to my office. I'll be along presently.

SPY: I'd rather wait in church if I may.

FIRST SOLDIER (*in disgust*): Church?

GENERAL Well, I'll find out in which establishment the bread is hardest, the water dirtiest, and liqueur least potent.

SPY: Thank you, thank you.

> As the TWO SOLDIERS *go, both façades rise.* HOOPER MOULS-WORTH *is alone and consults his watch. In the other Embassy,* VADIM ROMANOFF *is also alone, and also consults his watch. Both seem exasperated. Upstairs,* JULIET *is writing a letter, and choosing her words carefully, while* IGOR *is tying his sheets in complicated knots. The* GENERAL *enters the American Embassy.*

GENERAL (*beaming*): Not too early, I trust?

MOULSWORTH: I make you just on two hours late, but then I don't know the time around here any more than anyone else does. As it happens, it's not important as my Washington call seems to be delayed. Cigar?

GENERAL: Thank you.

MOULSWORTH: Now, let's come straight to the point. I talk blunt. When I want to know something, I just ask. That's the way I operate.

GENERAL: I appreciate that. In my position, I have to appreciate almost everything.

MOULSWORTH: Are you or are you not going to come into the Western community? I've got to know right now.

GENERAL: And how is your charming daughter?

MOULSWORTH: What's that? She's just fine, thanks. Just fine. Now if you're not going to play ball with us, just who are you going to play ball with, and why?

GENERAL: Yes. She looked exquisite last night, I thought.

MOULSWORTH: Who?

GENERAL: Your daughter.

MOULSWORTH: Didn't she though? Now lookit, no nation can afford to remain neutral these days, not with the bomb and economic pressures.

GENERAL: Who was that attractive young man she was with?

MOULSWORTH (*livid*): Leave him out of this.

GENERAL: Her fiancé perhaps? Will we soon hear the bells?

MOULSWORTH: No!

The telephone rings.

Oh, damn it! Excuse me. I thought I told you I didn't want to be interrupted . . . Who? (*Different voice.*) Washington? (*Ingratiating.*) Mr President . . .? Oh, just fine thanks . . . sure, she's fine too . . . Sure, and she's fine too . . . Just fine, all of us . . . I'm doing my damnedest, sir . . . I hope to have them wrapped up and in the Western community by nightfall. . . . Oh, sure, I've pointed that out . . . They've got a lot of pretty old-fashioned ideas . . . No, sir, I can't talk too freely right now . . . That's it, sir, that's the situation . . . Right here with me . . . Yeah, I'll do that, he'll appreciate it. . . .

The SOVIET AMBASSADOR *manifests considerable impatience in his room.*

Yeah . . . No, I don't need anything, sir . . . I'd be grateful if you could tell me the time, though, sir. Then I'd add six hours and fifty minutes, and know what time it is here . . . Is that right? Why, thank you, sir . . . (*He adjusts his watch while talking.*) O.K., sir, yes . . . And our fondest personal regards to Mrs President . . . Goodbye . . . (*With a sudden burst of laughter.*) Sure I remember the time . . . When I fell in the swimming pool with all my clothes on? . . . Sure, sure . . . had a hell of a lot of laughs . . . Goodbye . . . (*He hangs up.*) Great guy. Hey, you know something . . . you were two hours and forty-six mintues late.

GENERAL: And I thought I was ten minutes early.

MOULSWORTH: What were we talking about? Oh, before I forget it, Mr President sends his warmest good wishes for the financial prosperity of your nation.

GENERAL: Thank you, sir. And when you next telephone him, would you express to him my warmest good wishes for the financial prosperity of your nation.

MOULSWORTH (*no longer interested*): Sure. Thanks. Now—

GENERAL: We were talking about your daughter.

MOULSWORTH: We were? Hey, you noticed nothing ... nothing strange last night, did you?

GENERAL: With your daughter?

MOULSWORTH: Yes. Nothing ... visibly ... untoward?

GENERAL: No, except that she seemed radiantly happy.

MOULSWORTH (*weary*): Don't tell me, don't tell me. Those facts I don't retain. It's certainly a pretty exhausting life you lead us diplomats. Always celebrating, never an evening at home. (*Suddenly firm.*) We were going to discuss the Western community, weren't we, before you side-tracked me?

GENERAL: Not now, Your Excellency. You have pointed out yourself that it's very much later than we thought. I have to open a bridge half an hour ago.

MOULSWORTH (*very energetic*): I must have your answer tonight.

GENERAL (*elegant*): Perhaps we could find a moment to talk during the celebration?

MOULSWORTH: Celebration?

GENERAL: Yes, the Russians will accept, I feel sure.

MOULSWORTH: Another Independence Day?

GENERAL: Yes. Two as it happens. (*Awkward pause. Suddenly—*) Goodbye.

 He goes, leaving his portfolio and his gloves, and crosses swiftly to the Russian Embassy. The U. S. AMBASSADOR *finds the articles, makes to follow, then throws them down, and pours himself a whisky. The* GENERAL *enters the Russian Embassy.*) Not too early, I trust?

ROMANOFF: Only if I misunderstood the appointment, and it was for tomorrow.

GENERAL (*laughing*): I apologize.

MARFA *enters*.

ROMANOFF: What is it?

MARFA: Good afternoon.

GENERAL (*surveying her*): Good afternoon.

MARFA: Because of the defection of your habitual cipher-clerk, I have intercepted the message.

ROMANOFF (*takes a typewritten document*): Thank you.

MARFA *goes*.

Please excuse me.

GENERAL: Yes, of course.

ROMANOFF (*he reads quickly*): Now, I am directed to enquire of you whether or not you have decided finally to adhere to the Eastern Bloc.

GENERAL: How is your charming son?

ROMANOFF (*abrupt*): Not well. He will be leaving soon. It is imperative that we know by tonight.

GENERAL: He seemed to be throwing himself into the spirit of our national carnival.

ROMANOFF: It is a temptation which all of us must resist.

GENERAL: Otherwise you might become like us?

ROMANOFF: A sense of humour sabotages industrial development.

GENERAL (*laughs—then realizes that a joke was not intended*): He was with a very beautiful girl last night.

ROMANOFF: Please stick to the point. (*He consults the document.*) I see that the President himself has asked for your co-operation. I quote 'At any price' unquote.

GENERAL (*incredulous*): You know more than I do.

ROMANOFF: You must know that we tap your wires.

GENERAL: I know you do, but we don't. I always find a key-hole an unsatisfactory frame.

ROMANOFF: It depends on your possibilities. Once we have

taken the trouble to penetrate their codes, it is a pity not to benefit from the results.

GENERAL: Quite. It's like acquiring a degree, and then not practising. (*He rises.*) I hope to see you at our little celebration tonight.

ROMANOFF: My wife is very tired . . . so am I. . . .

GENERAL: The Americans have accepted.

ROMANOFF (*with a deep sigh*): We will be there.

GENERAL: Goodbye, sir.

ROMANOFF: Goodbye.

He leaves—without his walking stick. He crosses to the American Embassy. The SOVIET AMBASSADOR *finds the stick, puts it down absently, and pours himself a vodka. The* GENERAL *appears in the American Embassy.*

GENERAL (*genial*): I find I left my portfolio.

MOULSWORTH : And your gloves.

GENERAL: Those are not my gloves.

MOULSWORTH: No?

GENERAL: No.

MOULSWORTH: Oh. Drink?

GENERAL: No, thank you.

MOULSWORTH: Cigar?

GENERAL: Thank you. Incidentally, they know your code.

MOULSWORTH (*beaming*): We know they know our code.

GENERAL: Oh, really.

MOULSWORTH: Sure. We only give them things we want them to know.

GENERAL (*after a long pause in which the* GENERAL *tries to make head or tail of this intelligence*): Goodbye.

MOULSWORTH: See you. *And make up your mind!*

The GENERAL *leaves as the* U. S. AMBASSADOR *chuckles with pleasure. The* GENERAL *crosses to the Russian Embassy.*

GENERAL: I think I forgot my walking stick.

ROMANOFF: Here it is.

GENERAL: Incidentally, they know you know their code.

ROMANOFF (*laughing*): That does not surprise me in the least. We have known for some time that they knew we knew their code. We have acted accordingly—by pretending to be duped.

GENERAL (*after another incredulous pause*): I never realized before how simple my life was.

ROMANOFF: Remember. Tonight is the deadline.

GENERAL: Goodbye. (*He leaves and crosses to the American Embassy.*)

> ROMANOFF *sits sadly. Pause. The* GENERAL *enters the American Embassy.*

MOULSWORTH: Oh. Come right in. So you've come to sign, heh?

GENERAL: Not yet. I find on investigation that those gloves were mine after all.

MOULSWORTH: I thought they were. This life seems to be getting you down. Cigar?

GENERAL: Thank you. Incidentally, they know you know they know you know the code.

MOULSWORTH (*genuinely alarmed*): What? Are you sure?

GENERAL: I'm positive.

MOULSWORTH (*hearty*): Thanks. I shan't forget this.

GENERAL (*amazed*): You mean you didn't know?

MOULSWORTH: No!

GENERAL (*his majesty restored*): Goodbye.

MOULSWORTH: You haven't left anything?

GENERAL: No. Goodbye.

> *He goes and meets the* TWO SOLDIERS.

FIRST SOLDIER: We had to leave him in the church. We go on guard in half an hour.

GENERAL: I could do with a quick prayer myself. Cigar?

> *He puts one in his own mouth. All three light up and tiptoe out as the* TWO LOVERS *begin to let their sheets over the balcony. They see each other.*

JULIET: Igor!

IGOR: Juliet!
As their hands reach ineffectually for each other:

THE CURTAIN FALLS

ACT THREE

Evening to night.

*It is evening, and the stage presents a scene of imminent enchantment.
The street lamps are lit, and an elaborate gilt altar-piece has been
erected in the available space between the two Embassies. It is
evidently of considerable age, and its spiral columns of tawny gold
are lit by a host of candles. There are flags here and there. In the
distance, music, music for the open air, brass instruments and the
murmur of people.*

The TWO SOLDIERS *enter, in their uniforms, now more formal in
appearance. They carry two life-size papier-mâché figures of the
type used in religious celebrations. They have doll-like faces,
staring eyes, and are evidently either of great antiquity or else made
by most spontaneous and artistic peasant craftsmen. The front
views of these figures, one male, one female, have a weather-beaten
beauty, and are picked out in drab and subtle colours. On their
backs, however, are attached priceless robes of a former age, their
magnificence enhanced by their oldness. The* GENERAL *follows
the soldiers on. He is dressed in a uniform which hovers between
the exquisite and the ludicrous. Plumes, swords, spurs, the
rest.*

FIRST SOLDIER: Where d'you want them?

GENERAL: Here will do. (*He mops his brow.*) Everything in
place? The sheets? Yes. The letters! Attached to the sheets.
Splendid. There's so much to think about.

SECOND SOLDIER: The Archbishop didn't seem very pleased
at your suggestion, General.

GENERAL: A deaf Archbishop can be a nuisance, but tonight
he may have his advantages. Of course, he only became
Archbishop because he is entirely closed to the world of

sound. It gave him an austerity which visibly enhanced his capacity for meditation.

FIRST SOLDIER: Look out. Here he is.

GENERAL (*irritated*): He mustn't come here! We don't want to have to start shouting under the very walls of the Embassies.

But the ARCHBISHOP, *who is at least* 100 *years old and very small, approaches with a royal and terrible step. His train, which is of extreme length, and his mitre, which is of extreme weight, are being supported by our friend the* SPY, *now dressed in mauve rags, his head practically entirely occupied by an enormous tonsure, his eye brilliant with ecstasy.*

(*Ingratiating.*) My Lord Archbishop.

ARCHBISHOP (*who has a querulous but frightening voice*): General, this is an outrage! I have consulted many Holy books, and I find what I had indeed suspected, that the celebration of that most Royal Marriage between the Boy King Theodore the Uncanny and the Infanta of Old Castile does not fall until next Friday, and that tonight we celebrate our heroic participation in the Children's Crusade—so kindly have these invaluable symbols transported back to the National Museum with all dispatch.

GENERAL (*very loud*): Today is Friday.

ARCHBISHOP: Kindly stop mumbling.

GENERAL (*shouting*): Today is Friday.

ARCHBISHOP: You must speak up more.

GENERAL (*softly, to the audience*): I surrender. I tell him today is Friday, and——

ARCHBISHOP: Today Friday? Nonsense. Today is Wednesday the fourteenth. It has been since midnight.

GENERAL (*recovering from the shock—very, very softly*): Can you hear me now?

ARCHBISHOP (*irritated*): Of course I can hear you. If people wouldn't mumble so, I could hear everything.

GENERAL (*soft*): It's all the fault of the clock of St Ambrose.

ARCHBISHOP: What's wrong with the clock of St Ambrose?

GENERAL: Since it was built it has been losing time.

ARCHBISHOP: Losing time?

GENERAL (*normal*): Yes.

ARCHBISHOP: Mumbling again!

GENERAL (*very soft*): I beg your pardon. Yes. It has been computed by our Academy of Sciences that since thirteen eleven it has lost precisely two days.

ARCHBISHOP: The clock was not built in thirteen eleven.

GENERAL: It would have lost two days had it been built in thirteen eleven.

ARCHBISHOP: Gracious. Then it's Friday today.

GENERAL: Exactly.

ARCHBISHOP: Then we are not celebrating our contribution to the Children's Crusade at all.

GENERAL: No, we aren't.

ARCHBISHOP: What are we celebrating then?

GENERAL: The marriage between the Boy King Theodore the Uncanny and the Infanta of Old Castile.

ARCHBISHOP (*joining in*): Infanta of Old Castile. We shall then need the traditional altar of St Boleslav and the religious figures of the young couple for the symbolic wedding.

GENERAL: They are already in place. Now, if I may refresh your memory. Your Altitude . . .

    GENERAL *redirects Archbishop's attention to Altar and the two figures.*

ARCHBISHOP (*sees them*): My, my, how thoughtful of you. Verily, we have an efficient President at last.

GENERAL (*with some amusement*): I see, My Lord Archbishop, that you are well satisfied with the new convert I sent you.

ARCHBISHOP: To whom are you referring?

GENERAL: The Mauve Friar at your heels.

    The ARCHBISHOP *extends his hands with a smile. The* SPY *comes forward on his knees and is patted on his bald head, which he finds an elevating experience.*

ARCHBISHOP: He was admitted into the Holy Unorthodox

Church an hour ago, and was the only one to volunteer to
carry my mitre, which is of crushing weight, and my train,
which is of transcendent volume, on this great occasion. It is
disgraceful how lazy we are as a nation. Mark my words, he
will go a long way. Maybe, when I am gone—

SPY: No, no, no . . .

ARCHBISHOP: He has been absolved for one day from his
vow of silence, as he will help me with the ritual. Owing to
my extreme age, my memory has failed me, thank God,
before my heart or mind. I will prepare for the solemnities.

The GENERAL *and the* TWO SOLDIERS *bow as the* ARCHBISHOP
leaves with the overburdened SPY.

SECOND SOLDIER: Even if one doesn't approve of your
politics one has to admire you.

FIRST SOLDIER: I suppose so. (*He spits.*)

GENERAL: Boiled sweat would you care for?

The façades of both Embassies rise. The U.S. AMBASSADOR, *in
full tenue, enters. He is having difficulty with his tie.* BEULAH
follows in a violet evening dress. The upstairs rooms are empty.

BEULAH: I can't help you with your tie, Hooper, if you won't
stay still.

MOULSWORTH: I'm nervous. I've taken twelve vitamin pills
and I'm still nervous. How do you like that?

BEULAH (*working on his tie*): I wish we didn't have to go.

MOULSWORTH: For the thousandth time, Beulah, we just have
to go. A doctor is always on call. So's a diplomat. That pact
has just got to be signed tonight.

BEULAH: I never realized this country was so important.

MOULSWORTH: A casting vote is the important vote in any
board meeting. Where's Freddie?

BEULAH: He went out a lot earlier.

MOULSWORTH: What to do?

BEULAH (*blank*): Have some fun, he said.

MOULSWORTH: Fun. I'm glad he's not marrying Julie.
Positively glad. Have you finished?

BEULAH: Stand still.

MOULSWORTH: Has Julie eaten?

BEULAH: I put a tray by her door, but she just didn't answer.

MOULSWORTH: Goddam it, Beulah, you're heavy-handed.
The RUSSIAN COUPLE *enter.*

ROMANOFF: Evdokia, I asked you to help me with my tie.

EVDOKIA: Come here, into the light.

ROMANOFF: Where is that odious Comrade Zlotochienko? Every room I go into I expect to find her there, tapping wires, or thumbing her way though my papers.

EVDOKIA: She went out to do a social survey of living conditions here. She wants to lecture her crew when she gets home.

ROMANOFF: I don't envy them. And Igor? Has he eaten?

EVDOKIA: The loaf of bread I left by his door has not been touched. I knocked, but he was sulking.

ROMANOFF: Ow!

EVDOKIA: I'm sorry. I'm tired. I wish we didn't have to go.

ROMANOFF: It's my last manœuvre for Moscow. I might as well do it properly. Why do you look so sad?

EVDOKIA: I shall never be a grandmother.

BEULAH: There.

MOULSWORTH: Yeah. Feels good. Well. Time for a drink?

BEULAH: Hooper, you'd better not. Not after all those pills. Not if you have to sign a treaty.

MOULSWORTH: Guess you're right. Well. Got everything?

EVDOKIA: Finished.

ROMANOFF: Thank you. Now, shut your eyes.

EVDOKIA: What?

ROMANOFF: Shut your eyes, and don't turn round.

EVDOKIA (*resigned*): Are you going to shoot me?

ROMANOFF: We'll think of that tomorrow. (*He produces her beloved hat from a small box, and puts it gently on her head.*) You may open your eyes.

EVDOKIA (*whose fingers are feeling her head; with a shriek of joy*):
Vadim! The hat!

They embrace.

How could you?

ROMANOFF: I left and came back by the tradesman's entrance.

EVDOKIA: Oh, Vadim.

ROMANOFF: There. Let us go.

EVDOKIA: One more kiss.

MOULSWORTH (*about to exit*): I've been thinking, Beulah.

BEULAH: Yes, Hooper?

MOULSWORTH: How about a real good holiday soon? Just the two of us, like it was our honeymoon.

BEULAH: Hooper, d'you mean that?

MOULSWORTH: Never meant anything more sincerely in my life.

They kiss, too.

The Embassies close. The GENERAL *marches up and takes his position centre stage. The doors of both Embassies open, and both couples emerge at the same time. They bow coldly.*

GENERAL: Ah! How nice to see you here. The formal part of the celebrations are about to begin. Then afterwards we abandon ourselves to more profane pleasures.

FIRST SOLDIER: Regiment. Present—arms!

GENERAL (*sotto-voce*): Quite smart, but a little late. Try to remember next year ... (*Loud again*). Now, maybe a short historical résumé of the character of this Thanksgiving will not be entirely out of place. If you can find us on the map, and there are many, alas, who cannot, you will see at once that our position, geographically, militarily, financially, politically, administratively, economically, agriculturally, horticulturally, is quite hopeless. Consequently we have acted as a magnet to the invader throughout our long and troubled history. The English have been here on several occasions on the pretext that we were unfit to govern ourselves. They were invariably followed by the French on the pretext that we were unfit to be governed by the English. The Dutch made us Protestants for a while, the Turks made us Mahommedans, the Italians made us ... sing quite beautifully ... and these many centuries in close proximity to homesick and miserable soldiers has brought quick maturity to our men and babies of all colours to our women. ... The year 1311 was not a particularly eventful one in our history ... apart from the fact that the Albanians and the Lithuanians were both casting envious eyes on our territory at the same time, which rendered our traditional policy of balance of feebleness impractical. There was in fact an unwritten treaty between these two powers to split our land between them. The treaty was unwritten because at that period in history neither the Albanians nor the Lithuanians could write. The situation was further aggravated by the assassination of our Emperor, Thomas the Impossible, by an Albanian desperado disguised as a bunch of flowers. However, our Boy King came to our rescue and contracted a rapid Spanish marriage which brought Spanish troops to our assistance on condition we became Catholic. We did for a while until the Albanians and the Lithuanians decimated each other when we reverted yet again to the Holy Unorthodox Religion of our forefathers. It is this subtle trick which we celebrate today with much pomp and majesty. These are the symbolic figures, this of Theodore 1310-1311, Boy King. And this of Inez, the Infanta of Old Castile.

BEULAH: Isn't that interesting! I just adore history. It's so old.

MOULSWORTH: I wish there was some place to sit.

GENERAL: Ah! Silence please. The gentlemen will remove their hats.

The ARCHBISHOP *enters and stands before the Altar. The* SPY *follows on his knees, and squats by his side.*

EVDOKIA: By all that's holy! Do you see what I see, Vadim?

ROMANOFF (*unsurprised*): With him you can never tell if he's not still engaged in his old profession.

MOULSWORTH: Sh!

ARCHBISHOP: We are gathered here to observe in great solemnity the matrimony which saved our land on one of, alas, numerous occasions, from the savage heel of the invader. People of our country! Great powers to the east and to the west gird up their loins for war. Their regiments abound with Goliaths. We have only one David with which to oppose them—the Boy King Theodore the Eighth. He, in his wisdom and uncanniness, begs for the hand of Inez, the Infanta of . . . (*He dries up.*)

SPY (*softly*): Old Castile.

ARCHBISHOP: Old Castile. She accepts. The marriage which saved our fatherland is celebrated again. The tapestry of history unfurls. Let us . . . (*He dries up.*)

SPY (*consulting a document, softly*): Remember . . .

ARCHBISHOP: Remember the days of our distress. The bells are silent, the soil untilled, the fields barren . . . (*He dries up.*) What now?

SPY (*softly*): Come forth . . .

ARCHBISHOP: Oh, yes. Come forth, Theodore Alaric Demetrius Pompey, by the Will of the People Most Divine Protector of the Unwilling, Mentor of the Undecided, Emperor Absolute and Undisputed. Come forth, Inez Dolores Chiquita Amparo Conchita Concepcion Maria, Infanta Extraordinary of Old Castile, Hereditary Inheritor of Splendour, Purveyor of Wisdom, Holder of the Keys of Pamplona.

> *The* SOLDIERS *carry forward the figures and place them before the Archbishop, with their backs to the audience. Their absence from their original positions now reveals the sheets hanging from the balconies.*

BEULAH (*with a shriek*): Hooper! Julie's window! It's open.

MOULSWORTH: She's gone!

EVDOKIA: Vadim, the balcony!

ROMANOFF: He has escaped!

EVDOKIA: He's left a message!

BEULAH: She's left a message!

GENERAL: A little quiet, please. This is the most solemn part of the ceremony.

MOULSWORTH (*furious*): You must have known about this— why didn't you tell us?

GENERAL (*pointedly*): We never interfere with the internal affairs of other nations.

ROMANOFF: You mean you left these sheets dangling from our balconies for everyone to see?

GENERAL: Very few people pass by here. Now, silence, please!

ARCHBISHOP: The marriage will now be solemnized.

BEULAH (*who has read the message howling*): Julie! She's gone, Hooper! Gone to find her happiness with . . . . with *him*.

MOULSWORTH (*furious, to Romanoff*): You had a hand in this. (*To the General.*) I'll get you for this. I'll declare war. My only daughter.

EVDOKIA (*a scream*): Vadim . . . he speaks of suicide . . . life no longer holds anything without love or dialectic . . . wishes to die.

ROMANOFF (*frantic, to* MOULSWORTH): It's all the fault of your confounded daughter. My son, my son.

He kneels and weeps. EVDOKIA *throws herself on him. During this the* ARCHBISHOP *has been muttering.*

MOULSWORTH: I . . . I . . .

BEULAH (*screeching*): Hooper. *Do* something!

MOULSWORTH: Stop that man from talking first.

GENERAL (*loud*): The Archbishop is stone deaf.

ARCHBISHOP: Do you, Theodore Alaric——

MOULSWORTH: I'll get my car——

ARCHBISHOP: Demetrius Pompey——

MOULSWORTH: Search every—have the frontier sealed.

GENERAL (*indulgent*): Quiet, please!

ARCHBISHOP: By the Will of the People——

MOULSWORTH: Let me see that note.

BEULAH (*desperate*): It has no forwarding address.

ARCHBISHOP: Most Divine Protector of the Unwilling——

MOULSWORTH: I'll call Washington.

ARCHBISHOP: Mentor of the Undecided.

MOULSWORTH (*to General, fuming*): Call out the police!

ARCHBISHOP: Emperor Absolute and Undisputed ... (*He dries up.*) Yes?

SPY: Alias Igor Vadimovitch Romanoff.

MOULSWORTH: Hey, those figures have shrunk!

ARCHBISHOP: Alias Igor Vadimovitch Romanoff.

ROMANOFF: Igor!

ARCHBISHOP: Take this woman to be your lawfully wedded wife?

ARCHBISHOP: Do you, Inez Dolores—

MOULSWORTH: Stop the ceremony! It's a trick!

The SOLDIERS *bar the passage with their rifles.*

ARCHBISHOP: Chiquita Amparo——

ROMANOFF: Stop! Stop! Stop!

EVDOKIA: Vadim, why?

ARCHBISHOP: Conchita Concepcion——

MOULSWORTH (*to the General*): I'll have you bombed ... I'll summon the United Nations.

ARCHBISHOP: Maria, Infanta of Old Castile——

BEULAH: My girl, my girl.

ROMANOFF: We are impotent.

ARCHBISHOP: Hereditary Inheritor of Splendour.

MOULSWORTH: This calls for concerted action.

ROMANOFF: We have not the habit of collaboration.

ARCHBISHOP: Purveyor of Wisdom.

MOULSWORTH (*to General*): You have threatened the United States Ambassador——

ARCHBISHOP: Holder of the Keys of Pamplona——(*He dries up.*) Yes?

SPY: Alias Juliet Alison Murphy Vanderwelde Moulsworth.

ARCHBISHOP: Alias Juliet Alison Murphy Vanderwelde Moulsworth . . . I don't remember that in the ritual.

MOULSWORTH (*shouting*): Sure you don't! I said, sure you don't!

SPY: It is here, in illuminated letters of the fourteenth century.

ARCHBISHOP: Then it must be my memory again. Do you take this man as your lawfully wedded husband?

MOULSWORTH: No!

JULIET: Yes.

Beulah needs comforting—so does Evdokia.

ARCHBISHOP: I hereby pronounce you man and wife. Kiss your wife.

IGOR does so.

ARCHBISHOP: He is surprisingly mobile for a papier-mâché figure. Place the ring on her finger. Now go out there, my son, and beat the Albanians. Let the bells be rung.

The bells ring. A great shout of triumph rises from the populace. Fireworks begin to crackle. The married couple, who had substituted themselves for the wax figures during the discovery of the sheets, turn towards us, radiantly happy.

A miracle! Oh, well. That's quite usual here.

The ARCHBISHOP and the SPY leave, the SPY triumphant and laughing.

MOULSWORTH: It's not valid under American law.

ROMANOFF: It will not be recognized in the Soviet Union.

EVDOKIA: But Vadim—to see our son so happy!

IGOR: Father. Mother. May I present——?

JULIET: Dad. Mom. I want you to know——

The U.S. AMBASSADOR and SOVIET AMBASSADOR turn their backs. Shyly, BEULAH and EVDOKIA look at each other.

BEULAH: Why, Mrs Romanoff . . .

EVDOKIA (*emotional*): Comrade Moulsworth. . . . What are we to do? Isn't it always left to the women to make peace?

BEULAH: Why, yes, to see our children so happy . . .

MOULSWORTH (*sharply*): Beulah, I refuse to let you listen to that woman's peace feelers.

ROMANOFF (*sharply*): Evdokia, whatever you may have said and felt, we are Russian. You are walking into a capitalist trap.

A pause of indecision.

BEULAH (*precipitately*): Julie.

JULIET: Mother.

They embrace.

BEULAH: May I kiss Igor, and welcome him into our family?

IGOR: My second mother.

They kiss.

EVDOKIA: Igor!

IGOR: Mamasha!

EVDOKIA: And now let me welcome my new daughter.

JULIET: Oh, Mrs Romanoff . . .

They kiss.

MOULSWORTH (*who is dying to turn round*): Beulah, I shall not forget this. Your foolishness has cost me my job, my dignity, and my self-respect.

BEULAH: Hooper, darling, don't be so silly.

MOULSWORTH: You are condoning the actions of a government which has threatened your husband with loaded rifles.

GENERAL: Loaded? Only with blanks.

ROMANOFF: What?

GENERAL: Regiment. Into the air. Fire!

Two mild little shots, like caps.

GENERAL: Good.

MOULSWORTH: D'you mean to tell me . . . ?

GENERAL (*smiling*): We could only have acquired live ammunition by joining either the Western Community or the Eastern Bloc. We manufacture none ourselves.

JULIET (*appealing*): Pop.

IGOR (*appealing*): Pappa.

Pause. In a rush, the fathers embrace their children.

GENERAL (*triumphant*): From now on, we will no longer celebrate the marriage of our Boy King ... let the effigies rest in peace in the museum ... the Lithuanians and the Albanians no longer threaten anyone ... like us, they cling to existence with the claws of hope ... from now on and into the future, we will celebrate this, our greatest victory ... every year ... on the right day .... at the right hour ...

ROMANOFF (*suddenly*): Tell me ... why am I not unhappy? By the rule of prejudice, I should be overwhelmed with bitterness.

IGOR: You are not unhappy because I am happy, father ... and because we're in a happy country ...

ROMANOFF: I need proof of that. Happy? It can't be happy without a single factory, without a collective farm, without a communal centre.

FIRST SOLDIER: I thought that, too, Your Excellency—but tonight I wonder ...

MOULSWORTH: I don't get it, either, now we're talking about it. I ought to be just thunderstruck, just right in the throes of a breakdown, and yet I feel as though ... as though I'd just had a shower in champagne. (*He kisses his daughter.*) What's your subsoil like?

GENERAL (*pleasantly*): I haven't the slightest idea.

MOULSWORTH (*investigating the ground*): I bet it's lousy with oil.

GENERAL (*violently*): Then kindly leave it where it is. We only need to strike oil in order to be invaded tomorrow.

MOULSWORTH: Hey, some philosophy. Will you get that? A guy who doesn't want to own a Cadillac, on account of it's bound to be stolen.

JULIET: It makes sense to me, Pop.

MOULSWORTH (*laughing*): Already? You've been here too long.

BEULAH: May I compliment you on your hat, madame?

EVDOKIA (*blushing*): Thank you.

BEULAH: It's just darling.

ROMANOFF: I still need proof that I am legitimately happy—

IGOR (*amused*): Father, you're so didactic.

ROMANOFF (*severely*): So were you, yesterday. If we are to stay here—and obviously we cannot return to Moscow with any degree of safety—then I must know why I am so happy. Is it owing to a deeply frivolous nature, or is there something strangely, yet pleasantly, subversive in the very atmosphere of this place?

GENERAL: Ah, he's getting warmer. Isn't he, men?

SECOND SOLDIER (*with a sigh*): Yes, he is. It's in the air . . .

MOULSWORTH: Yeah. We can't return home either, Beulah. What can we tell the neighbours? So, we'll have to stay here for a while. But somehow—can't put my finger on the reason—but right now, I don't care. I don't care who signs which treaty with who. It's all way behind me—or maybe, it's way below me.

ROMANOFF: Yes—but speaking personally, I must know the cause. I must have proof.

The SPY *runs conspiratorially round the corner.*

SPY: Proof?

ROMANOFF: Have you been listening?

SPY: That is one habit I can never lose. If you want proof, hide —hide, quickly.

BEULAH: Where?

MOULSWORTH: Why?

SPY: Don't ask questions, and you will see. Hide, anywhere in the shadows.

He hides, too. The stage is peopled, but seems empty. Pause. The orchestra begins a waltz.

FREDDIE *and* MARFA *enter, obviously deeply in love. Gasps and whispers. A pause while they kiss.*

FREDDIE: Are there words which have not been used before?

MARFA: There are silences which have not been shared before . . . *They embrace.*

IGOR (*hotly*): They're using our words.

JULIET (*pained*): They've stolen our dialogue!

GENERAL (*gently*): It is our country which is talking through their hearts, as before it talked through yours.

JULIET: You mean we invented nothing of our own?

GENERAL: You invented everything—even the country which is yours.

MARFA: Why do you look at me so critically?

FREDDIE: Me? I never criticize anything, on account of I have no opinions.

JULIET (*affectionate*): Trust Freddie to break the spell.

MARFA (*coquettish*): No opinion at all ... then how do you know that you love me?

ROMANOFF: A logical question.

FREDDIE: I don't know, but I do.

MOULSWORTH: That's a pretty good blocking reply.

FREDDIE: Why do you love me?

BEULAH: Freddie's going right in there like a bulldozer.

MARFA (*a little sigh*): I don't know, either. I haven't any reason. I have every reason not to love you. You are a capitalist. (*Amorously*.) What do you manufacture?

FREDDIE: Refrigerators, washing machines, vacuum cleaners.

MARFA: What volume of laundry can you wash at one time with your largest model?

FREDDIE: I don't know.

MARFA: And how much dirt is needed to fill the bag of your lightest vacuum cleaner?

FREDDIE: I don't know.

JULIET (*irritated*): Oh, Freddie, try.

MARFA: You don't know ... perhaps ... perhaps I love you because you don't know ... it's such a relief ...

EVDOKIA (*delighted*): Ah, the disease is taking root.

FREDDIE: You're a ship's captain, aren't you?

MARFA (*with a sigh*): Yes ...

FREDDIE: Gee, that's great ...

MARFA: I'm captain of a sloop.

FREDDIE: Sloop. Sloop. That's a nice word. What's the tonnage?

MARFA: Why do you ask? You're not interested.

FREDDIE: No, that's right. I'm not. (*With a little laugh.*) I know what I like about you.

MARFA: What is it—(*Recklessly.*)—my love?

FREDDIE: Let me finish what I got to say, and then I'll kiss you. Of all the girls I've ever known you're the only one who could possibly be a captain of a ship.

MARFA: The only one?

FREDDIE: My mother, she could have been an admiral—but you, you're the only one who could have been captain of a ship.

MARFA (*her eyes shut*): I'm waiting.

FREDDIE: One other thing. How about you and me getting married?

MARFA: You're practical. I like that.

FREDDIE: I'm a capitalist.

MARFA: I hardly know you.

FREDDIE: That's why I ask you so soon.

MARFA: What would you do if I accept?

FREDDIE: I'd be very surprised.

MARFA: I accept.

FREDDIE: I'm very surprised.

    They kiss with increasing passion.

SPY: Proof enough?

    In silence, HOOPER *kisses Beulah,* VADIM *kisses Evdokia.*

JULIET: I'm jealous of them already. I want it all to begin again.

IGOR: With all our agony?

JULIET: Oh, that was nothing . . .

    They kiss, too.

GENERAL (*to the audience*): It is the night. Our victory is won. Do visit our country, if you can. The fare is as cheap as walking to the corner of the street to post a letter; accommodation is magnificent. All you need do is to shut your eyes, and in the night, with tranquil minds and softly beating hearts, you will find us here . . . the realm of sense, of gentleness, of love . . . the dream which every tortured modern man may carry in his sleep . . . our landscape is your pillow, our heavy industry—your snores. . . .

He retires in the darkness, and blows out the candles on the Altar. The music is a lullaby. The four love scenes continue in silence.

FIRST SOLDIER: D.

SECOND SOLDIER: R.

FIRST SOLDIER: D.R.E.

SECOND SOLDIER: A.

FIRST SOLDIER: D.R.E.A. . . . Oh . . .

SECOND SOLDIER: Ah . . .

FIRST SOLDIER: M.

SECOND SOLDIER: One—love.

CURTAIN

NOTES

PAGE

9   Da, golubchik. . . . Paidi Suda. . . . Sichas (Russian):
      Yes, my little dove. . . . Come here. . . . Presently.

14   *Marx:* The works of Karl Marx (1818-83) were the gospels of
      Russian Communism. Marx and Engels wrote the *Communist
      Manifesto* in 1847-8 and after the Revolution in 1848 Marx was
      expelled from Prussia. He settled in London, where he wrote
      his major work, *Das Kapital.* His grave is in Highgate.

18   *Trotsky:* Leon Trotsky (1879-1940) was Lenin's ablest collabora-
      tor in the Revolution of 1917, the creator of the Red Army and
      a hero of the Civil War. Juliet has heard of him as one of the
      founders of the Soviet regime; but she evidently doesn't know
      what happened to him later. After Lenin's death in 1924 he
      fell out with Stalin, was expelled from the Party, and went into
      exile. He became the regime's most hated critic. He was mur-
      dered in Mexico in 1940. Igor's generation would regard him as
      a worse enemy than any capitalist, and the name *Trotskyist* is
      still used in condemnation of traitors to the Cause.

      The General tactfully suggests that Juliet was confusing
      Trotsky with *Engels.* Friedrich Engels (1820-95), the life-long
      friend and collaborator of Marx, is still revered.

19   *Orpheus:* It was by looking back that Orpheus lost his Eurydice.
      She had died and gone down to Hades, but he followed her
      and persuaded the authorities (by his enchanting music) to let
      her return to the world of the living, on condition that he did
      not look back to see if she was behind him. He did not resist the
      temptation, and so lost her for ever.

23   *The fault, dear Brutus . . .* Cassius in Shakespeare's *Julius Caesar*
      says 'The fault, dear Brutus, is not in our stars, but in ourselves.'

23   '*a guy who sent a food-package to the wrong side in Spain*': During
      the Spanish Civil War (1936-9) sympathy with the Left-wing
      Government in its struggle with Franco's Fascist rebellion was

quite respectable, but in later years might be recalled as evidence of Communist leanings. Most food packages went to the Left.

27 *St Petersburg:* founded by Peter the Great in 1703, was renamed Petrograd in 1914 and again renamed Leningrad in 1924. It was the capital city of the pre-Revolution Russian Empire.

27 *Cossacks:* Cossack troops were the traditional bulwarks of the Tsarist regime, used to suppress strikes, riots, and rebellions. The *knout* (a kind of whip) is associated with savage punishment of offenders; it was also used by the Cossacks in suppressing riots. The Cossacks were largely neutral in the March rising which overthrew the Tsar, but in the October Revolution they were against the Bolsheviks. The latter were strongly supported, however, by rebel warships and thousands of armed sailors who came ashore.

29 *Winter Palace:* The Winter Palace in St Petersburg was the stronghold of royal and aristocratic privilege and wealth until the Romanovs (i.e. the Tsar and his family) were ousted. In the October Revolution it was shelled by the Bolsheviks because the Provisional Government had headquarters there. Thus it is associated with the enemies of Communism.

30 *Saboteur! Interventionist! Anarchist! Trotskyist!:* These are all common words in the Communist vocabulary of vituperation. Anybody who does not entirely support you can be accused of sabotage (i.e. throwing a spanner in the works). It is less appropriate to call your enemy an Interventionist, though it is understandable that the word is a powerful term of abuse; for when the Revolution was over Russia had to suffer three bitter years of Civil War intensified by the intervention of foreign powers, including Britain, U.S.A. and France. *Anarchists* and *Trotskyists* were denounced even more bitterly than capitalists and interventionists, on the principle that the man who is closest to your ideas is the worst traitor and the most dangerous wrecker if he will not conform.

34 *Barricades:* in the language of the Class War the barricade is thought of as the front line in the final street fighting, when it becomes clear whether a man is for the workers or against them. Martyrs are assumed to be on the workers' side.

36 *Princeton:* One of the old-established universities of the U.S.A.

45 *Honoured Artist K. K. Bolshikov:* Not, of course, a real person.
     Ustinov is making fun of the propagandist plays of the time
     which were uncritically accepted because they suited the
     regime.
54 *Liqueur:* Some religious communities have been famous for
     making liqueurs, e.g. Grande Chartreuse.